Foreword by Edwina P. Allen

ℛOARING
𝒜LL 𝒯HE 𝒟AY ℒONG

When

PROPHETESS O.W. PETCOFF

Roaring All The Day Long: When
Book One in the *Roaring All the Day Long* Series
2nd edition

Copyright © 2024, 2001
ONOMA Ministries & Publications
First Printing 2001
ISBN:0-9701184-0-6/978-0-9701184-0-0

Scripture quotations are taken from the
Holy Bible, King James Version
Copyright © 1996, Thomas Nelson, Inc.

Definitions are taken from
The New Strong's Exhaustive Concordance of the Bible
James Strong, LL.D., S.T.D.,
Copyright © 1996, Thomas Nelson Publishers

Webster's Seventh New Collegiate Dictionary,
A. Merriam-Webster,
Copyright © 1971 G. & C. Merriam Co.

Published by:
ONOMA Ministries & Publications
Arlington, Texas
omonpee.petcoff@outlook.com

Cover illustrations by Elijah Tan.

Dedication

This book is dedicated to my grandmother,
Mrs. Mary Lee Brewer.
Although you have gone home to be with the Lord, the
things that you imparted to me will always be with me.
I love you, Grandma, and I miss you so very much.

Acknowledgements

I would like to begin by thanking God for the grace and strength for this undertaking. I am honored that He, The Omnipotent Creator of All Existence, would bestow upon me the awesome responsibility of teaching His People.

Next, to Ron, my husband, I say, "Thank You"; I love you very much. I sincerely appreciate all the sacrifices you made to enable me to bring this book into fruition. I am proud to be "Mrs. Petcoff"; I am blessed to have you in my life.

To my children — Monisa and Desmond — I say, "I love you!" You, too, have sacrificed your "quality time" with Mommy during the making of this project. I appreciate both of you for being the sweetest, most loving children a mother could ever have.

To my mother, Mrs. Ledora Beard, thank you for all your help throughout the years. Your being who you are has helped me to become who I am.

To Pastor Sonja Russell Bogan of LoveJoy Outreach Ministries in Metropolis, IL, I thank you for teaching me to hear God. With all that you have poured into me prophetically, I have no doubt that you will see a little of yourself and your teachings in the pages of this book.

To Edwina P. Allen, I say thank you for inspiring in me the courage to try again. Your input in this project inspired me tremendously. Rest in peace, beautiful Woman of God.

To my sister, my friend, my intercessor, and my confidante, Adrian Thornton. I cannot even begin to mention all the ways in which you have been a blessing in my life. I will just say thank you for editing this manuscript. Your keen eye for detail coupled with your loving me enough to push me to "get it done" was just what I needed. I love you, Sis!

To Charles and Emily Webster, my dear friends who I met after the first printing of this book: I love and appreciate you all so much. We were Divinely connected and have been friends ever since. Thank you so much for all that you have done for my family and me. Above all, thank you for loving me and hanging in there with me.

Finally, to each and every one who has helped me throughout the years, please know that you are not forgotten. Although time and space will not allow me to mention each one of you by name, you are forever in my thoughts and prayers.

Table of Contents

Foreword — *vii*

Preface — *viii*

Introduction — 1

Chapter One:
THE WHEN OF PROPHETIC INQUIRY — 6

Chapter Two:
THE WHEN OF TEMPORARY LACK — 11

Chapter Three:
THE WHEN OF PROPHETIC PRECISION & TIMING — 21

Chapter Four:
THE WHEN OF PROPHETIC PARADIGMS & PATTERNS — 32

Chapter Five:
THE WHEN OF ABUNDANT GRACE & MERCY — 37

Chapter Six:
THE WHEN OF ALTERNATIVE MEANS — 61

Chapter Seven:
THE WHEN OF PROPHETIC CONDITIONS & MANDATES — 75

Chapter Eight:
THE WHEN OF SPIRITUAL RESURRECTIONS & CONTINUATIONS — 99

Chapter Nine:
IN PURSUIT OF THE WHEN — 114

Conclusion — 138

Notes & Reflections Pages

Foreword

Dear Friend,

These are the encouraging words I promised I would do for your book series. I pray that this is just a "selah" to what God really has for you.

In reading this book and sharing with you about the focus of this series, I am reminded of a security blanket.

"Why a *security blanket*," you ask? The purpose of a security blanket is to shield us from something; it is presumed to have the ability to protect. A security blanket warms us when we are cold and shields us from light. Sometimes it is used simply to make us feel comfortable.

We tend to associate security blankets with young children, who hold on to them as a means of alleviating some unknown fear. However, I have found that security blankets are used by people of all ages. I have also found that security blankets come in different forms. This includes both physical and spiritual security blankets. When we reach a certain "age" in Christ, we should no longer seek an additional source of security because we have reached a maturity level at which we rely on Christ to become our *security*. We then realize that it is God who is our "*blanket*"; our *covering*; our *protector*.

I thank God that you have finally found Him — God — to be the one in whom you find refuge during times of insecurity. I love the God in you and pray His Protection over you throughout this project.

Sincerely,
Edwina P. Allen

Preface

*P*lease be advised that this series of books was written by a highly anointed Prophetess of God; one with an intensely Prophetic word for a chosen Prophetic People who have a predestined Prophetic purpose. All others are certainly welcome to read this but should be advised that the revelations divulged within these pages will produce life altering aftereffects. Your thought processes will be changed. You will not be afforded the pleasure of looking at even the simplest things in life in the same way ever again. Your spiritual senses will be heightened, causing you to experience unusual sensations at the mere mention of the Prophetic. You will also experience seemingly unquenchable cravings for the deeper revelations of the Word of God. I tell you right now that, as author, I will not be held responsible for the aftermath that is sure to ensue after you read this powerful book...nor will I take credit for it. For, in Hebrews 4:12, the Bible declares the following:

"...the word of God is quick, and powerful, and sharper than any two-edged sword, piercing even to the dividing asunder of soul and spirit, and of the joints and marrow, and is a discerner of the thoughts and intents of the heart."

And, again in **Isaiah 55:11:**
"So shall my word be that goeth forth out of my mouth: it shall not return unto me void, but shall accomplish that which I please, and it shall prosper in the thing whereto I sent it."

Once we've been exposed to the true and unadulterated Word of God, as one of my favorite TV quotes states, "resistance is futile."

Prophetic People — prepare to be challenged, enlightened and enhanced. **All Others** — You're welcome to continue; you've been duly informed of the consequences.

Formalities aside, the *"Roaring All The Day Long"* series (or *"Roaring"* series) is a microscopic view of **Psalm 32:3** and explores the silencing or constraint of a gift or calling. The source scripture — Psalm 32:3 — states the following:

"When I kept silence, my bones waxed old through my roaring all the day long."

This series offers comprehensive spiritual insight and revelatory intricacies surrounding some causes of spiritual repression, frustration and stagnation, - particularly in the lives of prophetic people. This book — *When* — is the first book in the *Roaring* series is based on the first word of Psalm 32:3. It identifies various spiritual seasons (*whens*) and gives insight as to who and when to move within and glean from these seasons, thereby causing the Divine Purpose for our lives to come into fruition.

To this point, I have given a general overview of the series. I will now give a more specific description of that this series entails. But, because of the intensely prophetic nature of the material, it is difficult to explain specifically what this series addresses without first explaining what it does not.

Psalm 32:3 was written by David after his affair with Bathsheba. The story of David and Bathsheba is a familiar one in which David, smitten with Bathsheba, arranges for her husband to be sent to the front line of battle, where he is killed. Traditionally, when this story is taught, it is always taught along the premise that David — a man after God's own heart — committed adultery and had a man killed; but then David repented. The fact that someone of David's spiritual stature could commit acts of sin and fall short of the glory of God serves as a reminder for each of us to be mindful of our spiritual state *("Wherefore let him that thinketh he standeth take heed lest he fall."* – **I Corinthians 10:12**). The concept of being spiritually aware is certainly important but **is not** the focus of the series.

The fact that David was a man after God's own heart is often skimmed over. Having a heart after God meant that David desired nothing more than to do the things that were pleasing and edifying to God. He delighted in praising and worshipping God. David loved God with his whole heart, so much so that later in the scriptures, the Bible says that David danced before the Lord so mightily until his clothes fell off (**II Samuel 6:14**). David stands as a paragon of love and adoration for God; the paradigm of a true worshipper and praiser. However, David's praise and worship **are not** the focus of this series.

How traumatic it must have been for David, who had been so intimate with God, communing with Him daily, to have committed an act of sin. It was one of which he was so ashamed, he would not share it with anyone, especially with God (i.e., *"When I* **kept silence…** *"*). He kept it inside and did not divulge it until such time as God sent the prophet Nathan to David with a Word that convicted him of his wrongdoing (**II Samuel 12:1-14**). David experienced deep conviction as a result of his sin. Nevertheless, David's conviction **is not** the topic of this series.

Even with a great man of God such as David, the Bible declares that it is sin that separates us from God (**Isaiah 59:2**). David, who had been anointed to serve as King of Israel; David, who loved God with all his heart and soul; David, a man after God's own heart — found himself in a place where he could no longer feel the presence of God in the same way. In this place, the anointing that had been bestowed upon him was still present, but did not flow as freely or with as much ease — his sin had produced a *spiritual constriction*. Consequently, the sin, when held in and not released (**"When I kept silence"**) began to penetrate his very being, causing deterioration of his spiritual foundation. That is to say, he would pray but could not hear from God. He would worship and praise but could not enter into God's presence. His foundation (**"[his] bones"**) became corrupt and he experienced a spiritual "osteoporosis"; i.e., **"[his] bones waxed old"**. The act of "holding it in"; the not releasing what was inside of him caused extreme frustration, lack of spiritual intimacy with God, and had he not released it, would have ultimately resulted in his spiritual death. But, God allowed David to feel an excruciating discomfort and would not allow him to become complacent in his unrepentant condition. Instead, God allowed David to enter into a spiritual state where his inner being warred within itself (another example of similar warring can be seen in **James 4:1**). This state of warring became so intense that it took on a personification, even having a "voice". The "voice" was so loud until David perceived it as a **"roaring"**; a roaring that was constant and unrelenting; a **"roaring all the day long"**. This **"roaring"** — *the intense struggle and process to release what is inside of us — particularly prophetic gifts, ministries and impartations* — **is the focus of this series**.

What has God placed inside of **you** that is roaring to come forth? And why haven't you **released** it? There are many reasons why we suppress the things of the Lord and allow the *roaring* to begin in the first place. Personally, this series was birthed out of my *roaring*. The spirits of rejection and persecution, the lack of prophetic mentorship and other factors contributed to the *roaring* in my life.

For years, I went through spiritual repression and frustration, afraid to be who God called me to be. I was afraid of the reactions of those around me. I was called of God as early as 5 years old but was not ordained as a minister until I was 15. Even as a teenager, I knew beyond a shadow of a doubt that God had a great calling upon my life. Wanting to "fit in" with the crowd, but never really being able to do so, I suppressed the gift of the Prophetic and the calling to the office of the Prophet. I hoped and prayed that someone — *anyone* would accept and appreciate me.

Yes, God would bless me to have moments of release; I would minister a Prophetic Word here or sing praises there.

Nevertheless, each time, the enemy would make sure that my same old nemeses — Rejection and Persecution — would be right there to torment me. They would come namely in the form of "Church Folk", who had neither an understanding of nor a calling to the Prophetic. It became a vicious cycle that eventually wore me out. Not having the strength to fight anymore, I stopped trying. As I became an adult, the Lord blessed me to find a place — LoveJoy Outreach Ministries in Metropolis, Illinois — in which I was taught the "basics" about Divine revelation. However, the Lord had even more in store for me.

The Lord blessed me to get married to a wonderful Christian man and move to Texas, still hurt and bruised from childhood scars. However, I found the same spirits of rejection and persecution running rampant in the churches in that particular area. Disappointed and tired of trying, I retreated into my own little world for a span of about five years. I still had a relationship with God; I still received Prophetic revelations but was not willing to fellowship with any one body of Believers (in my mind, *Me + Church Folk = Hurt*). Nor did I want to share what I received from the Lord with anyone, for fear of being rejected or ridiculed. I had a singular goal in mind: I did not want to preach or, for that matter, hear anyone else preach. I did not want to prophesy. I certainly did not want to write a book. **My goal**, I concluded, **was simply to be left alone**. And, as for my goal, I would have achieved it, too…. **had it not been for that confounded roaring!**

The *roaring* was the thing that kept me awake all night, pondering the things of the Lord, although my flesh did not want to do so. It was the force that kept driving me and would not let me be complacent, although I purposed in my heart not to go one step further in ministry. The *roaring* was the thing that would not let me commit suicide, even at my lowest point because somewhere deep inside me I knew that there was great ministry and enormous worth. It was the gnawing and pulling in my spirit toward revelatory teachings and messages. The *roaring* was the unquenchable desire to fulfill God's Divine Purpose for my life; unquenchable because nothing else would fill the void. Nothing else would make me happy or give me peace. **Nothing short of fulfilling God's Divine Purpose for my life would stop the roaring.**

So, through a series of events (some to which I will refer throughout the series), I made up my mind to stop the *roaring*. I began to actively seek to do God's Will and fulfill His Divine Purpose for my life. The *roaring* has subsided because the ministry, which was once trapped within me, is now freely flowing out of me and into the lives of other Believers. My "**bones**", though they still ache from years of neglect, are no longer "**waxing old**"; I am now free.

In Luke **22:32**, the Bible says, "*...and when thou are converted, strengthen thy brethren*"; writing this series of books is my first step toward doing just that.

With each word that I write, I am silencing the *roaring* in my spirit. I am being taken to another level in God, one in which Prophetic revelation is increased and the promises of God are made manifest. It is a place of awesome power; a place of infinite joy; a place of unending spiritual growth (*"from glory to glory"*). Come — *Prophetic People and All Others* — and go with me to that place through the pages of these books.

Introduction
(or, It's Only *When*…RIGHT?)

*F*irst and foremost, let me say that I *did not* intend to write a book about *when*.

When God told me to write a book, I knew that the book would be part of a series. I also knew that the title of the series would be *Roaring All The Day Long*. However, I did not know what the subject matter of any book in the series. I went ahead and obeyed God. Like the depiction of Abraham in Hebrews 11:8, I "went out, not knowing wither [I went]" in my pursuit of this series of books that would be known as *The Roaring Series* and would focus on Psalms 32:3, which reads:

When I kept silence, my bones waxed old through my roaring all the day long.

As I continued to seek the mind of God for direction, a highly prophetic and well-trusted friend and I were discussing the issue. After having written what I thought was to be *Chapter 1: When*, I gave the then 12-page manuscript to my friend to edit. As she and I were discussing her editorial suggestions, she unknowingly prophesied, "*This* chapter *is* your book!" That statement struck a chord in my spirit and I knew instantly that God was speaking to me through my friend. He was telling me to take those twelve pages and allow Him to expound upon what He had already given me because the entire subject of this book was to be based upon the meanings of one word: *when*.

If you are like me, you are asking yourself the same question that I asked God when He instructed me to write this book in this manner. Specifically, you are wondering, "Why in the world would anyone write (or read) a book about **when**?" I continued to inquire of the Lord, saying, "What's the point? After all, it's not a complete sentence. It's not even a phrase or fragment. It's only **when**."

"Lord," I said, "**when** is such a small, seemingly insignificant part of the English language; a monosyllabic word that consists of a mere four letters. It doesn't tickle the ears. It commands no notable degree of attention when uttered. Lord, truthfully, the word **when** is really rather boring. Its, well…it's only **when**!"

"Furthermore," I continued, "why **when**, Lord? I mean, of all the words that you could have chosen for me to write about, why didn't you choose a more prestigious, eloquent word? Why not choose *ostentatious, celestial*, or even *epiphany*? Why not some grandiose word that has flair and distinction; something that resonates of academia or high culture? Please, Lord, " I asked in desperation, "won't you reconsider? There is no way I'll find anything else to say about THAT word. After all, it's only *when*."

But, to my chagrin (at that time), God did NOT change His mind. This time He spoke **directly** to me and reiterated what He had spoken through my friend; this book was to be about *when*. God then told me to read I Corinthians 1: 27-29. These three verses are as follows:

But God hath chosen the foolish things of the world to confound the wise; and God has chosen the weak things of the world to confound the things which are mighty.

And the base things of the world, and things which are despised, hath God chosen, yea, and things which are not, bring to nought things that are:

That no flesh should glory in his presence.

God then asked me, "What makes the 'foolish things' seem foolish? And what makes the 'weak things' seem weak?" As I contemplated the answers to these questions, God continued speaking:

"The answer to both questions is that in each instance there is a **lack of revelation as to the Prophetic purpose and to the potential of the 'things'**. It is, in fact, a matter of perception more so than the true worth of the things being considered that would make them appear foolish or weak. Because the 'wise' and the 'mighty' think that they are self-sufficient, they rely upon their own knowledge, intellect, strength and ability. Therefore, they do not see the need to seek My Help. They are comfortable in their own ability to 'figure things out' and 'get things together'."

"The 'wise' and the 'mighty'," God continued, "pride themselves on their 'internal' resources and do not develop the disciplines of consulting Me or being attentive to My Voice. In their way of thinking, what would be the need? They take no heed to the scripture which admonishes them to ".... lean not to thine own understanding" (Proverbs 3:5b). They take the simple things (i.e., the 'foolish' and 'weak' things) for granted, neither seeking nor receiving the deeper revelations as to their purposes. And, in doing so, they overlook a wealth of *prophetic gold mines; revelatory diamonds in the rough.* They inadvertently discard and disallow spiritual treasures that come packaged in the 'plain brown paper wrapping' of commonality and insignificance…just like the word *when*. Do not be like the 'wise' and 'mighty'; open your spirit and receive even more revelation about this simple word so that I might birth this book through you."

And suddenly, it all made sense to me. As I opened myself to the possibility that a book *could* be written about *when*, God poured out revelation upon revelation. I slowly but surely came to understand *why* God told me to write *The Roaring Series* and why *when* was to be the subject of the first book of the series. I realized that understanding our prophetic *whens* is paramount to stopping the *roaring* in the life of every Believer. It is the first step on the journey into our Divine purposes and destinies.

While on the surface, it's still "only *when*", after I received God's Revelation, I can now look beyond the surface and see that this small, insignificant word proves to be so much more — a life-changing, yoke-destroying, powerfully prophetic principle. But, in order to fully appreciate the magnitude of "when", we must first understand what a prophetic *when* is and how it impacts our lives.

WHAT IS A *WHEN*?

During a church's African American History Celebration, two beautifully anointed women of the Lord performed a hilarious skit entitled "Storytelling." They portrayed two sisters, sitting around the kitchen table after church on Sunday (as is the custom in African American households), talking about "the way things used to be". Each time one of them reminisced about "the good ol' days", she always started out with, "Remember *when*…?"

It is fitting that *when* is the first word of Psalm 32:3 - the series' source scripture. David used this word to begin speaking of a bleak, despairing time in his life. This was a time of utter loneliness and desolation, in which he — "a man after God's own heart" — had lost the close fellowship with God that he had previously. In this verse,

David was acknowledging his agony. He was reflecting upon his bad times. David was remembering his *when*.

We, too as a Prophetic People, must learn to detect our spiritual *whens*. But, what is a *when*?

According to one definition of **when** in the Miriam-Webster Seventh edition dictionary, in its noun form a **when** is "a time in which something is done or comes about". This definition applies to physical/chronological *whens* but is also true of spiritual *whens*. God speaks to us through every situation and circumstance in our lives. However, it is up to us to be attentive to His Voice (Rev. 2:7 declares "He that hath an ear to hear, let him hear what the Spirit [of God] saith unto the churches [us]"). Therefore, we must also be in tune with what is taking place in the spirit realm. From the very foundations of the earth, God has divinely orchestrated events and occurrences in the life of every Believer to usher us into our Divine Purpose. In turn, each of these events and occurrences has been assigned a certain season in our lives. Each season has been meticulously configured by God and strategically placed at a certain time in our lives that God knows that it will be the most effective in achieving His desired result. Now, whether or not we are aware of these seasons does not change the fact that they will occur. And, to be honest, until we grow to a certain level of spiritual maturity and awareness, we often do not realize that there has even been a season until the season has passed! These seasons are our spiritual *whens*.

This book — *When* - explores prophetic revelations about our spiritual *whens*. *Chapters One thru Eight* each discuss a different spiritual *when*. The premise of each of these chapters is derived from a definition of the word *when* taken from the Merriam-Webster Dictionary. *Chapter Nine* discusses recognizing, naming, embracing and remembering our spiritual *whens*.

1

The When of Prophetic Inquiry

𝒯he first definition of *when* listed means "*at what time.*" Although it is used to make statements (example, "He will return *when* he gets ready."), this *when* is often used to ask questions and is an adverb. Adverbs are used to modify (or tell about) verbs. Verbs are action words. So, in effect, used while asking a question, this *when* asks "At what time is (an) action going to take place?" This *when* is the *When* of Prophetic Inquiry.

Every Believer will experience this *when*, a season in which we ask questions of God; specifically, we ask Him *when* something is going to happen. "**When** will I be married? *When* will my ministry take off? *When* will I get a promotion? **When** will my finances be increased? **When**, Lord, **when**?" I'm sure that if we would be honest, we could think of times in our lives when we have asked God, "**When**?" And, certainly, there is nothing wrong with asking God when He is going to do what we are believing Him to do. Because we are His Children and He is our Father; because "it is in Him that we live and move and have our being"; because we are a Prophetic People who depend upon His every utterance for our mere existence, it would stand to reason that we desire and need to know *when* His promises and blessings are going to manifest.

WORD JUNKIES

So, clearly, desiring to know **when** is not wrong. But, we must be careful not to become engrossed in or obsessed with wanting know **when**; always seeking a prophetic word from the Lord regarding the timing of events in our lives. God showed me that, in the past few years, there has been a trend in the church toward the gift of the prophetic, specifically as it pertains to personalized/customized information for individual Believers. People who may not even attend church on a regular basis will flock to see someone who supposedly flows in the gift of the prophetic and/or who allegedly walks in the Office of a Prophet. God said that this, in and of itself, is not bad, except that many of these people are not coming to praise and worship Him. They are not interested in hearing the message or in learning what is being taught. Sadly, He revealed to me, their primary focus is to get an answer to *"When, when, when*?" They take no heed to Matthew 6:33, which says, *"But seek ye first the kingdom of God and his righteousness; and all these things shall be added unto you."* All they want is to "receive a word." Such people can best be depicted as "Word Junkies".

Itching Ears

It is this Word Junkie mentality — the "itching ears" of which II Timothy 4:3 speaks — that has infiltrated the church and resulted in other problems. Specifically, a spirit of complacency has crept into the Body of Christ. Because of this mindset, many people have simply lost the desire to seek God for themselves. Instead of studying the Bible, praying, fasting and doing whatever else it takes for them to get an answer from God for themselves, it becomes more convenient (and, in a sad way, more entertaining) for them to be singled out in a crowd, have hands laid upon them and be prophesied to by a Man or Woman of God. When a spirit of complacency is prevalent within a body, the people often do not want to hear the preached or taught Word. All they want is to see the *manifestations* of the Word — the signs and wonders.

Moreover, it is this ungodly, overwhelming yearning for signs and wonders (i.e., "Tell me *when, when, when*") that exploits the gift of the prophetic and the Office of the Prophet. In fact, this yearning practically relegates them to the level of a three-ring circus— "the bearded lady, the clowns, the dancing bears…and the Prophet." Not only does this ridiculous mentality make a mockery of the gift of the prophetic and the Office of the Prophet, but also it spiritually prostitutes them, perverting the very purpose for which the prophetic manifestation was intended.

Looking back on it now, I can admit that this is one of the very things that caused my *roaring*. It sent me spiritually running, yelling and screaming away from the church and into my own little world. Having been called to the Office of a Prophet at an early age, I moved in the gift of the prophetic as far back as I can remember. However, I really had no one to teach me about such things. With my not having anyone in my life that could help me understand my calling, it was years before I was spiritually mature enough to withstand and effectively deal with people's desire to see the manifestations of my gifts. I could not handle being pulled upon and being set out on display — all this, not for the glory of God (although that was how it was explained to me), but for the entertainment and personal benefit of people. All because these people wanted to know "*When, When, When?*" and did not want to do what it took to get an answer from God for themselves.

Psychic Phenomena

Another by-product of the Word Junkie mentality is the increased interest in psychic phenomena and occult-related activities. People are so driven by their desire to know "*when?*" until they seek the assistance of so-called psychics to give them a reading to predict their future. They also turn to satanic activities as a means of ascertaining the information they seek. The saddest part of these scenarios is that it is not just the unsaved who are partaking in these activities, but those who profess to be Christians as well. The obvious danger in this is the possibility of being drawn into activity that will ultimately lead to demonic oppression and destruction. Saul was a perfect example of this:

> *Then said Saul unto his servants, Seek me a woman that hath a familiar spirit, that I may go to her, and enquire of her. And his servants said to him, Behold, there is a woman that hath a familiar spirit at Endor.*

> *And Saul disguised himself, and put on other rainment, and he went, and two men with him, and they came to the woman by night: and he said, I pray thee, divine unto me by the familiar spirit, and bring me him up, whom I shall name unto thee. – I Samuel 28:7–8*

> *So Saul died for his transgression which he committed against the Lord, even against the word of the LORD, which he kept not, and also for asking counsel of one that had a familiar spirit, to enquire of it;*

> *And enquired not of the LORD; therefore he slew him, and turned the kingdom unto David the son of Jesse. – I Chronicles 10:13-14*

The *When* of Prophetic Inquiry is a season in which we learn the benefits of patience *("But let patience have her perfect work, that ye might be perfect and entire, wanting nothing." – James 1:4).* We also experience the results of waiting *("But they that wait upon the Lord shall renew their strength; they shall mount up with wings as eagles; they shall run, and not be weary; and they shall walk and not faint."* – *Isaiah 40:31*). The *When* of Prophetic Inquiry drives the serious Believer into the next realm of spiritual maturity. It increases one's faith in God and prepares us for the next level of warfare. It is in this *when* that we learn to trust God more, thus asking *"When?"* less. We are no longer doubtful of His promises and rest in the assurance that what He said — sooner or later — is going to come to pass. Our fears dissipate and our *"When?"* becomes *"Whenever."*

2

The When of Temporary Lack

*T*he next definition of *when* is "*at a former and usually less prosperous time.*" It has to do with a past time in which things were uncomfortable, difficult, and painful. An example of this usage of the word *when* is, "Oh, sure, he's rich now, but I knew him *when.*" During this season, things were not as good as they are presently. In fact, our past situation has changed so that we are now bettered and have "lived to tell the tale". This time of hardship — this season of trials and tribulations — is the *When* of Temporary Lack.

The word *lack* means, "to be wanting or missing; to be short or have need." Personally speaking, this is a *when* with which I am well familiar. Honestly, if there is one thing about which I can testify it is what it feels like to do without; to have a need. And, I might add, not only have I lacked material things, but I have gone without emotional and spiritual needs being met as well.

Interestingly, I have learned from many seasoned men and women of God who have a prophetic anointing, that experiencing the *When* of Temporary Lack is almost a "prerequisite" of a prophetic ministry. This *when*, they tell me, is a spiritual rite of passage into the deeper realms of the prophetic. Perhaps this is because it is during this *when* that we come to know God as Jehovah Jireh — "*The Lord is Our Provider*", understanding that, no matter whatever we lack, He has already provided it by His Word. We come to trust God more in this *when* and understand that He will not allow us to be tempted any more than we are able to bear (I Corinthians 10:13). We no longer trust in our own ability to provide for ourselves (*i.e., the leaning not to our own understanding* spoken of in **Proverbs 3:5**). Instead, we learn (even if our learning is through "trial by fire") to put our needs and desires aside, and search for the deep revelations of His Word. That is, we want to know *why* we are in this situation and *what we must learn* in order to be released from this place.

REASONS WHY WE LACK

God said that we are now in a dispensation in which we must understand *why* we lack. He said that this is especially true for prophetic people. In fact, He said, there are times during which He literally assigns seasons of lack to our lives to achieve certain goals. He then showed me an example of this in my own life.

When we first got married, my husband and I experienced our share of financial difficulties. Having both grown up in upper-middle class families, prior to adulthood neither my husband nor I had ever lacked for any material possession. Yet, for the first few years of our marriage, we struggled to pay for necessities like food, clothing utilities and shelter. And, for the most part, "extras" were out of the picture. To make matters worse, one week after we were married and living in the Midwest, God had spoken to us and commanded us to pack up and move to Texas, away from everyone and everything that we had ever known. At that time, we knew only one family in Texas, and they lived more than 20 miles away from where God had instructed us to settle.

Although God never allowed us to go hungry or be homeless, it can be safely said that anything else that we could lose (outside of our family), we lost it during this time. The furniture that we brought to Texas began to deteriorate rapidly the moment we moved it into our apartment. Within a matter of months, the clothing that we brought with us would no longer fit, and, with limited finances, we could not afford to replace our wardrobes. Then, the brand new car my husband bought me as a wedding gift mysteriously broke down. But, again, with finances being low, we would have to drive the car in its state of disrepair, thus exacerbating the problem until the car eventually became un-drivable. With inadequate clothing and no transportation, it became at times virtually impossible to either find or maintain employment, which made the financial problem even worse. This affected our ability to even pay the note on the car that we couldn't drive to get to jobs that we didn't have and for which we couldn't dress appropriately if we had them! It became a vicious cycle of lack, despair and loss. We had no one to which to turn…. That is, no one but God.

During this time, God drew us closer to Him. We learned to depend on Him as never before because we were now more cognizant of our need for Him than we had ever been. During this *When* of Temporary Lack, there was no "Mamma", no "Daddy"; no family name or money like that to which we had previously been accustomed. There was God, and that was all there was! Even with my college education and reputation as an overachiever, God had placed me in a position in which I could not climb the corporate ladder. I could not call in a favor from one of my many well-connected acquaintances back home. *I could do nothing but lie on my face and call out to Him* and depend upon Him for day-to-day survival.

As I prepared to write this chapter, God showed me that He used that time to teach me at least five essential principles about lack and why He allows it to affect the lives of Believers. These principles are as follows:

1. Lack - once rectified — yields glory to God.

Ultimately, God said, He allows us to be in places of desperation so that He can get the glory out of our triumph. Consider the following story from John 9 in which Jesus and His disciples happen upon a blind man:

> *And as Jesus passed by, he saw a man which was blind from his birth.*
>
> *And his disciples asked him, saying, Master, **who did sin, this man, or his parents, that he was born blind?***
>
> *Jesus answered, Neither hath this man sinned, nor his parents: **but that the works of God should be made manifest in him.** — John 9:1-3*

As is the case with human nature, the disciples wanted to know *why* the man was blind. Given the phrasing of their question (verse 2), they had concluded that man's blindness (i.e., his *lack* of sight) must have been a direct result of sin, either on his part or on the part of his parents. Jesus assured them that the man did not lack his sight as a punishment for sin. Instead, Jesus told them, God allowed the man to be born blind because He had ordained that very moment they were experiencing — the moment in which Jesus would heal the man and God would be glorified. God allowed a situation of lack so that ultimately He would receive the glory for the miraculous outcome.

Likewise, God puts us in situations where there is literally no other way out than through trusting Him. As with my own personal testimony, we exhausted every means of rectifying our financial problem that we could think of, but to no avail. But, because of God's Divine Purpose for our lives and our ministry, He allowed us to go without. He ordained that season so that when He commanded the lack to cease and the promised prosperity to begin, we, and others who "knew us *when*" would *have to* give Him glory.

The apostle Paul came to understand and relish the concept of lacking so that God would get the glory from a victorious outcome. In II Corinthians 12:9-10, Paul writes the following:

> *And he* **[God through Jesus Christ]** *said unto me, My grace is sufficient for thee: for my strength is made perfect in weakness. Most gladly therefore will I rather glory in my infirmities* **[lack of well-being]** *that the power of Christ may rest upon me.*

2. Lack yields a breaking down of the flesh.

A popular old saying states, "Man's extremity is God's opportunity." What this old saying means is that, in times of adversity, when man has done all that He can do, he must humble himself and rely on God to do the rest. A second reason that God allows lack is to show us how limited our own abilities are, but how powerful He is and to teach us that, without Him, we can do nothing.

Lack produces suffering. And, according to the book *Understanding the Flow of the Anointing,* written by Dr. Sherman C. Gee Allen, suffering yields character. In *Chapter Five: The Relationship of The Anointing to Leadership,* Dr. Allen expounds upon various spiritual laws. Dr. Allen coined one such law "The Law of Progressive Manifestation." He explains, "Each element of spiritual progress yields with it a spiritual manifestation." He further teaches why suffering, an element of spiritual progress, yields the manifestation of character (or, honesty with self). Dr. Allen writes the following:

"Through suffering, we allow ourselves to experience the hardships and unpleasant circumstances of which Christ partook. Through suffering, we begin to take on the mind of Jesus, which results in character being established." [1]

Moreover, in keeping with Dr. Allen's thoughts, character — *honesty with self* — must then result in a deeper God-consciousness. That is, if I am honest with myself, I must admit that, after having done everything within my limited ability, I yet need God. What I am in effect doing at this point is "demoting" my flesh, and exalting God. I am coming to see my flesh for what it really is — a physical entity through which God must get glory. I therefore no longer follow the dictates of my flesh but rely solely on the mandates of God.

Forasmuch then as Christ hath suffered for us in the flesh, arm yourselves likewise with the same mind: for he that hath suffered in the flesh hath ceased from sin:

That he no longer should live the rest of his time in the flesh to the lusts of men, but to the will of God.
– I Peter 4:1-2

3. *Lack forces us to discover hidden anointings, talents and gifts.*

Hailing from a rich southern heritage, my mother could always come up with some "interesting" sayings. One of my favorites was when she would humorously say, "Old NeedMo' will make you do things you said you couldn't do!" What she meant by that is "Old NeedMo[re]'" — *lack personified* — drives you to a place where you are forced to be creative. Sometimes God allows us to lack because He wants us to discover our hidden anointings, talents and gifts.

When I was a child, we attended a small FreeWill Baptist church. Membership was small, so it always seemed that only a few people did most of the work. Because we lacked "manpower", I was called upon to serve in many capacities, some of which rather came naturally to me (singing the choir, for instance). However, I was also asked to serve in capacities with which I did not necessarily feel comfortable with at first (such as teaching Sunday School). But, because there was no one else to do it, I "stepped up to the plate." And, consequently, because there was no one to teach me how to do this, I had to pray and ask God to show me how to teach. When I prayed, God began to reveal the scriptures to me in a way that, to that point, I had never heard anyone else teach them. God then showed me that I had a knack (an anointing, a talent and a gift) for spiritual teaching. Because of lack, I discovered the teaching and speaking styles and abilities that He placed within me, both of which I still use to this very day.

A Biblical example of this principle is Nehemiah. While serving as the king's cupbearer (Nehemiah 1:11), Nehemiah heard that "*the remnant*" of the Jews "*that [were] left in captivity*" were "*in great affliction and reproach.*" He also heard that the wall and gates of the city of Jerusalem had been destroyed (Nehemiah 1:3). It grieved Nehemiah, who himself was a Jew, to see his people in such distress. Upon hearing the news, Nehemiah immediately prayed and asked God to help him. Nehemiah felt the call to lead his people to restore the wall of the city.

Although he had no experience in such matters (serving as a cupbearer to the king), Nehemiah understood that there was no one else who would accept the challenge of doing this, so, *because of a lack of anyone else to do so*, he undertook the challenge. He was granted permission by the king (Nehemiah 2:1-8) and, with much prayer, organized and supervised the rebuilding efforts (Nehemiah 6:15).

4. Lack creates an atmosphere in which we feel compelled to pray.

James 4:2c says, *"...yet ye have not, because ye ask not."* This portion of the verse implies that while God desires to bless us, we are unable to receive the blessing because we will not pray. A fourth reason why God allows us to lack is because He wants us to feel compelled to pray. In our praying, we are initiating a dialogue with God in which we are relaying to Him the sincere desires of our heart. We are humbly requesting His assistance in areas of our lives. When we pray, we open a door for God to heal our lack and to do a great work in our lives. The practice of praying is vital to our Christian Walk and helps to make us victorious in our Christian living. Unfortunately, at times, we become complacent and neglect to pray. Therefore, because God loves us, He creates a situation in which we do not know all the answers and we do not know how to help ourselves — *He creates a situation of temporary lack.* As a means of seeking relief from this chaotic state, we remember that we can pray to God and He will answer. Scriptural examples of the importance of prayer include the following:

> *And he spake a parable unto them to this end, that men ought always to pray, and not to faint. – **Luke 18:1***

> *Pray without ceasing. – **I Thessalonians 5:17***

5. Lack makes us specific in our prayers.

In addition to creating an atmosphere in which we feel compelled to pray, lack also forces us to be specific in our prayers. As we learned in the previous principle, it is important to pray. However, James 4:3a teaches that although we may pray, *"[we] ask, and receive not, because [we] ask amiss."* Therefore, we can conclude that it is not enough merely to pray. In fact, God requires that we as a Prophetic People reach a level of spiritual maturity at which we are specific about what we pray. Because of this, He sometimes allows us to go through a period of lack that is so intense until we find ourselves almost "dissecting" every word of our prayers. We will learn to make sure not to pray the wrong thing.

Jesus believed so strongly in the importance of praying correctly until He left us a prayer paradigm. This paradigm — found in Matthew 6:9-13, listed below — shows us the manner in which to pray so that God will answer our prayers.

After this manner, therefore pray ye: Our Father which art in heaven, Hallowed be thy name.

Thy kingdom come. Thy will be done in earth, as it is in heaven.

Give us this day our daily bread.

And forgive us our debts, as we forgive our debtors.

And lead us not into temptation, but deliver us from evil: For thine is the kingdom, and the power, and the glory, for ever. Amen.

TEMPORARY LACK

The *When* of Temporary Lack is potentially the most painful *when* we will encounter. However, it is important to remember that this season is, after all, temporary. Although we are experiencing hardship right now, once God has completed His work in us for this season, we will no longer experience this lack. Or, as Psalm 30:5b says:

"...weeping may endure for a night, but joy cometh in the morning."

---

1. Dr. Sherman C. Gee Allen, *"Understanding the Flow of the Anointing,"* (Fort Worth, TX: Charity Book Publishers, 1999). pp. 61-63

3

The When of Prophetic Precision and Timing

*T*he Bible declares, *"To every thing there is a season, and a time to every purpose under the heaven"*. **(Ecclesiastes 3:1)**. As we mature prophetically, we no longer merely desire to hear God's voice. We become keenly in tune with the Holy Spirit and God's prophetic timing. We then receive the revelation that, at this realm of our understanding, God is requiring a specific action in a specific manner within a specific time span. During such times in our lives — the *When* of Prophetic Precision and Timing — God teaches us to be precise in our obedience to Him, or to move when He says it in just the exact way He says.

How often has God told you to do something that you did not do, but later wished that you had? Or, how often has God told you to do something in a specific way, but you in your "wisdom" decided to do it differently, only to find out that God's way was really the *only* way? During the *When* of Prophetic Precision and Timing, God teaches us to perform on command. We learn to follow His instructions "to a 'T'", knowing that disobedience will neither be allowed nor tolerated. We come to realize that the slightest hesitation in or deviation from following His instructions can yield disastrous results. It is during this *when* that we must acknowledge (and, later learn to appreciate) the fact that as Believers, every action we take has been predestined. Or, as Psalm 37:23a says, *"The steps of the good man are **ordered** by the Lord...."*

ORDERED STEPS

Psalm 37:23a is a scripture that is often quoted and used as a text for sermons. I, too, have quoted it often and have used it to speak of God's love for His People and His assurance that, no matter what we go through, it will be okay because He has "ordered" our steps. It is for this reason, I concluded, that God took time to meticulously and painstakingly "order" — *or arrange in specific sequence or chronology* — each and every step we will ever take. This is certainly true, but as I began to write this section, God gave me a deeper revelation concerning His ordering of our steps. Specifically, God showed me the word *ordered* and revealed two key definitions of the word.

The first use of the word *ordered* is the one to which I previously alluded. It means, "to arrange in specific sequence or chronology." We must be ever cognizant of the fact that, even before the foundations of the earth, God had great plans for our lives. To ensure that those plans would come into fruition, God charted a course that we must take. This course will lead to His Divine Purpose being fulfilled in us. Having entrusted such a great responsibility to us, God knew that we could not do this alone. Like any loving father, God cares for our success and wellbeing, so He paved the way for us to have life and that more abundantly (John 10:10b); to be blessed in the city and in the field (Deuteronomy 28:3). He prepared a means by which we can fulfill His Divine Purpose for our lives. He "stacked the deck" in our favor by "arranging" circumstances and events in our lives to occur at key moments, triggering the necessary responses and reactions. The responses and reactions then combine to achieve God's expected end for an appointed season. So, in effect, by God "ordering" our steps, He also ordered our *whens*. That is, God arranged (ordered) for us to be at designated points, experiencing specific events (steps), during specific seasons (*whens*). He did this because He had something specific planned for us *when* (i.e., "Just At The Moment That" or during the *When* of Prophetic Precision and Timing) we are in the right place at the right time!

The notion of God ordering our steps (i.e., arranging them) for our benefit is encouraging. However, God showed me that there is a much more powerful yet rudimentary reason for God's ordering of our steps. But, for us to comprehend and appreciate this reason, we must first understand a second definition of the word *ordered*. In this definition, *ordered* is defined as "commanded". Therefore, in this scenario, God has *commanded* our steps. "But", one might ask, "*why* would God *command* our steps?"

In every instance in the Bible, when God issued commandments, He spoke things into existence. This is because whenever God speaks, He speaks a *creative word*. In fact, Jesus — *God in the Flesh* — attested to this prophetic principle in John 6:63 when He said, "…[T]he words that I speak unto you, they are spirit, and they are life." God's command causes that which was not, to materialize. God spoke to the elements and the "worlds were framed" (Hebrews 11:3). He spoke to darkness and the darkness gave way to light (Genesis 1:3). Again, through Jesus, God spoke to Lazarus and immediately the once dead Lazarus came back to life (John 11:43-44). *God's commandments are creative because they come out of the very spirit of God and because they are His Word.*

Therefore, when God *commanded* our steps, He spoke His Word over all events that will ever occur in our lives. He did so, not necessarily because He loves us or He wants to bless us (although He does), but the primary reason that God spoke His Word over us is *to bring into fruition His*

Divine Purpose for our lives. Now, the Bible declares in Ezekiel 12:25 that God watches over His Word to perform it. What this means is that whatever God speaks, not only is it going to come to pass, but God Himself is going to *personally* supervise it (by watching over it). He does so to make sure that the outcome is pleasing to Him and that the desired affect is achieved. Therefore, if God *commands* our steps, He has spoken specific mandates for those steps, commanding them to be taken in the direction, sequence and pace that will lead to the fulfillment of His Divine Purpose in our lives. Consequently, if His Divine Purpose is fulfilled in us, then His Word is manifested through us (because the Bible declares that His Word shall not return unto him void, but shall accomplish that which it was set forth to do [Isaiah 55:11]). And, because we know that heaven and earth shall pass away, but His words shall not pass away (Matthew 24:35) and it is impossible for God to lie (Hebrews 6:18b), we know that God has made every provision to ensure that His Word performs that for which it was intended. Because He said it, He must do it. Because we are His people, He will do it through us.

This is why the embracing of the *When* of Prophetic Precision and Timing is so crucial in the lives of Prophetic People. We must be sensitive to the voice of God and take heed to every Word that He speaks. Those who are serious about following God must move in a realm of spiritual discipline that is like unto a military mentality. The Commander-in-Chief (God) gives specific instructions. We, the soldiers, must carry out the orders — no questions asked. And, in keeping with the military analogy, we must understand that failure to follow orders may result in serious disciplinary action.

In this *when*, we learn to be detail-oriented, knowing that there is a specific purpose for every command that

God gives us. For instance, if God says to pray, we understand that we must find ourselves praying, no matter how early or late the hour. Then, once we receive the mandate to pray, we must then sharpen our spiritual senses and ascertain the specifics: For whom or what are we praying? With what frequency are we to pray? Each time we are in prayer, how long should we pray? Where should we pray? If we are to see a manifested move of God in our lives, we must follow God's mandates as specifically as possible.

During the *When* of Prophetic Precision and Timing, we learn to "…be *instant, in season and out of season;…*" (II Timothy 4:2b). We are to be ready to obey the command of the Lord (instant) both when we know what to expect (in season) and even when we don't have an inkling of what God is doing in our lives (out of season). We come to understand that our steps are indeed ordered, and we begin to walk by faith and not by sight (II Corinthians 5:7). This, in turn, makes us surefooted in our relationship with God. We become confident that wherever the journey takes us, it will ultimately lead to our places of Prophetic Purpose and Destiny.

My favorite scriptural example of the *When* of Prophetic Precision and Timing is the story of the transfer of Elijah's anointing to Elisha. The story is as follows:

And it came to pass, when the Lord would take up Elijah into heaven by a whirlwind, that Elijah went with Elisha from Gilgal.

And Elijah said unto Elisha, Tarry here, I pray thee; for the Lord hath sent me to Bethel. And Elisha said unto him, As the Lord liveth, and as thy soul liveth, I will not leave thee. So they went down to Bethel.

And the sons of the prophets that were at Bethel came forth to Elisha, and said unto him, Knowest thou that the Lord will take away thy master from thy head today? And he said, Yea, I know it; hold ye your peace.

And Elijah said unto him, Elisha, tarry here, I pray thee; for the Lord hath sent me to Jericho. And he said, As the Lord liveth, and as thy soul liveth, I will not leave thee. So they came to Jericho.

And the sons of the prophets that were at Jericho came to Elisha, and said unto him, Knowest thou that the Lord will take away thy master from thy head today? And he answered, Yea I know it; hold ye your peace.

And Elijah said unto him, Tarry, I pray thee, here; for the Lord hath sent me unto Jordan. And he said, As the Lord liveth, and as thy soul liveth, I will not leave thee. And they two went on.

And fifty men of the sons of the prophets went, and stood to view afar off: and they two [Elijah and Elisha] stood by Jordan.

And Elijah took his mantle, and wrapped it together and smote the waters, and they were divided hither and thither, so that they two went over on dry ground.

And it came to pass, when they were gone over, that Elijah said unto Elisha, Ask what I shall do for thee, before I be taken away from thee. And Elisha said, I pray thee, let a double portion of thy spirit be upon me.

And he said, Thou hast asked a hard thing: nevertheless, if thou see me when I am taken from thee, it shall be so unto thee; but if not, it shall not be so.

And it came to pass, as they still went on, and talked, that, behold, there appeared a chariot of fire, and horses of fire, and parted them both asunder; and Elijah went up by a whirlwind into heaven.

And Elisha saw it, and he cried, My father, my father, the chariot of Israel, and the horsemen thereof. And he saw him no more: and he took hold of his own clothes, and rent them in two pieces.

He took up also the mantle of Elijah that fell from him, and went back and stood by the bank of Jordan:

And he took the mantle of Elijah that fell from him, and smote the waters, and said, Where is the Lord God of Elijah? And when he also had smitten the waters, they parted hither and thither: and Elisha went over.

*And when the sons of the prophets which were to view at Jericho saw him, they said, The spirit of Elijah doeth rest on Elisha. And they came to meet him, and bowed themselves to the ground before him. – II **Kings 2:1-15***

As I meditated upon this passage of scripture, God revealed several key reasons why Elisha was successful in receiving the anointing of Elijah. God said that the following revelations are tantamount to our learning not to miss Him during the *When* of Prophetic Precision and Timing:

1. **We must be in the right place at the right time.** *(verse 1)*
II Kings 2:1 tells us that, at the time that Elijah was to be taken away, Elisha was with him. One of the reasons that Elisha was successful in receiving the mantle is that, even from the beginning of his relationship with Elijah, Elisha was always in the right place at the right time. God said that during the *When* of Prophetic Precision and Timing, it is important for us to be in the right place at the right time. We must be in the place — physically and spiritually — where we can receive what we are to be receiving at that time.

2. **We must be determined.** *(verses 2 and 4)*
Because Elisha was determined to receive from Elijah, he swore to him three times, saying, *"As the lord liveth, and as thy soul liveth, I will not leave thee."* Elisha understood that in order to receive the mantle, he had to be determined.

Likewise, God is saying that we, too, must be determined to receive from Him during our *Whens* of Prophetic Precision and Timing. Although we may be in the right place at the right time, if we are not determined to receive, we may miss what God has in store for us during this season. We fall prey to the "the-spirit-is-willing-but-the-flesh-is-weak" mentality, which is erroneously derived from Matthew 26:41b. In this often-quoted-but-commonly-misunderstood passage of scripture, Jesus was speaking to Peter. Ironically, in using that scripture to justify our actions when it comes to something we don't want to do, we conveniently forget to quote the first half of the verse in which Jesus said, *"Watch and pray, that ye enter not into temptation"*. What Jesus was saying was that Peter, too, would have to be determined to finish that season. In fact, Peter would have to be so determined to finish until he denied his own fleshly needs and desires and began to watch and pray.

3. *We cannot listen to any voice other than God's, no matter who it comes from and especially if it sows seeds of negativity and doubt.* *(verse 3)*
Elisha would not allow the sons of the prophets to talk with him about Elijah's departure. Elisha loved Elijah and would miss him greatly, so did not want to hear what these men would say, because dwelling on the situation would make him grieve. He knew that, because of the seriousness of the hour, he would do himself a great disservice to succumb to emotions. That is, he had to remain "sharp" and stay focused on what God was doing in this hour.

We, too, must learn the prophetic discipline of tuning out every voice around us that is not saying what God wants us to hear in that season. Too often, we listen to people who are well-meaning but ignorant. These people do not understand that they are saying things that are, in fact, detrimental to our spiritual well-being and survival during that season in our lives. We must remain spiritually on-point and know that we are in a season in which it is too crucial to miss what He is saying to us.

4. *We must be specific in that for which we ask God.* *(verse 9)*
Elisha knew exactly what he wanted from Elijah — "a double portion" of his anointing. We, too, must pray specific prayers during the *When* of Prophetic Timing and Precision. As we discussed in *Chapter Two: The When of Temporary Lack*, praying the right prayer is crucial. Moreover, understanding what God wants us to pray is equally as important. We must come to a place of spiritual maturity in which we "let this mind be in [us], which was also in Christ Jesus" (Philippians 2:5). Then, as we allow

our minds to become like His, we understand His Will for us. As a result, we come to understand what to pray.

5. *We must receive specific instructions and follow those instructions as completely as possible. (verses 9 and 10)*
In order to obtain what he requested, Elisha had to receive and follow specific instructions. God said that during the *When* of Prophetic Precision and Timing, He teaches us to receive and adhere to stringent instructions. He creates an atmosphere that is like a "prophetic boot camp" in which God (again, the Commander-in-Chief) gives specific commands to His Drill Sergeant — the Holy Spirit. The Holy Spirit, in turn, relays those instructions to us, the enlisted men. We, the enlisted men, must then comprehend and follow those instructions as completely as possible.

6. *We must exert an effort to receive from God; although it is promised, we must "take it up" (verse 13).*
Shortly after Elijah was taken away, Elisha stood there gazing at the sky, longing for Elijah. It occurred to him, however, that upon Elijah's departure, his *mantle — symbolic of Elijah's anointing and, therefore, Elisha's promise —* had fallen to the ground. Upon regaining his composure, Elisha located the mantle and "took it up" from the ground. When he did so, he literally took his blessing in his own hands.

I have heard this scripture taught as if Elisha *caught* the mantle, but, as we can see, the Bible clearly says that Elisha "took it up". That is, even after he had done everything he knew to do (principles 1 thru 6), he was yet expected to exert an effort to receive his promise.

God said that too often we expect our promise to "fall into our laps". Nevertheless, during this *when*, God teaches us that we must put forth the effort to go get what God has for us. In doing so, we show God that we recognize the promise and are willing to do what it takes to receive it.

7. *We must demonstrate our skill in using the thing gained from the when (verse 14).*

Elisha understood that there was great power in the mantle. He demonstrated this power by putting on the mantle and smiting the water, causing it to separate. God said that during the *When* of Prophetic Precision and Timing, we must know how to use what He gives us to glorify Him. We must be willing and able to demonstrate that we understand the purpose for which He gave us the blessing obtained during this *when*.

4

The When of Prophetic Paradigms and Patterns

kin to the *When* of Prophetic Precision and Timing (Chapter Three) is the *When* of Prophetic Paradigms and Patterns. Although both are based on the premise of "ordered steps", their objectives (or lessons to be learned) are different. The *When* of Prophetic Precision and Timing teaches us to "walk on command." It designates a direction to a destination that is often undisclosed. The *When* of Prophetic Paradigms and Patterns teaches us to detect paradigms and patterns in our "steps."

Ecclesiastes 1:9 is based on the concept of this *when* as it decrees that "the thing hath been, it is that which shall be; and that which is done is that which shall be done; and there is no new thing under the sun." During this *when*, God reveals His mysteries and "formulas" to those who are in tune enough with His Spirit to receive them. Because of the intensely revelatory nature of this *when*, all Believers will experience this season, but only the Chosen, Prophetic Believer will glean from it. Because "that which is born of the flesh is flesh; and that which is born of the spirit is spirit" (John 3:6), successful completion of the *When* of Prophetic Paradigms and Patterns will only be experienced by Believers who have cultivated an intimate relationship with God and who commune intimately with Him on a frequent basis. The Believer who is able to flourish in this *when* will be a person who is completely sold out to God and prays without ceasing (I Thessalonians 5:17). Additionally, the Believer will possess and flow in a strong gift of discernment. Having become mature in his or her gift of discernment, the Believer can then "rightly divide" the *whens*. This Believer can therefore take a microscopic view of each *when* to determine what the repetition of various actions and events indicate about his or her life. Any Believer who gleans from this *when* must use spiritual insight to determine what God is doing in them or saying to them at the present, based on the results of similar experiences in the past.

"BEHOLD, THE DREAMER!"

Like the Biblical character of Joseph, one of the ways that God deals with me is in the realm of prophetic dreams. Having been entrusted with a gift of interpretation of dreams, I often have detailed dreams that are symbolic of important events and spiritual landmarks in my life. Years ago, I began having dreams in which a dear childhood friend would appear. Although the dreams were infrequent, as I began to understand prophetic revelation, I knew that God was trying to speak to me. As I matured in the gift of the prophetic, I understood that this friend would appear in my dreams during times in which I was about to make an important choice in my life. I came to understand that this was the simplest way that God could relay to me what He was trying to tell me about various decisions in my life, even though the interpretation of these dreams often proved to be somewhat puzzling. Nevertheless, I accepted God's way of speaking to me in this manner. Every time after that, when I had a dream in which the friend appeared, I understood that I was in "decision" mode. However, I did not realize until later that, in each instance in which the friend appeared, God was trying to reveal something *different* to me about the decision that I was going to make. Specifically the friend represented God (i.e., *"A friend loveth at all times...."* [Proverbs 17:17a]); *"...and there is a friend that sticketh closer than a brother* [Proverbs 18:24 b]). Whenever the friend appeared frowning, God was telling me "no." But, when the friend appeared with no expression, God was telling me to wait. After receiving this level of revelation, I was no longer content in merely knowing that when this friend appeared, God was trying to tell me something. I now knew exactly what was being said and how to handle each situation.

God revealed even more prophetic symbolism pertaining to the friend in my dreams: Was the friend standing or sitting? Where was the friend in relation to me (beside me, behind me, in front of me)? What color was the clothing that the friend wore? Through prayer, meditation and consecration, I developed a discipline in which during my dreaming period I "step outside of myself" and am both a participant in the dream and a third-party observer. As the observer, I am taking notes, ascertaining all the prophetic symbolism within the dream sequence so that when I awake, I can meditate on the information and receive the full revelation of what God was saying to me.

I learned to do this because I understand that although I recognize and remember similar *whens*, I know that there is yet something different that God wants me to receive from each dream experience. That is why (as we will discuss in *Chapter 9: In Pursuit of the When*) the same type of *when* will occur more than once in our lives, but at different times will have different "names." I therefore came to realize that, because of the different lessons to be learned, in order to move into the deeper realms of the spirit to which I aspire (and to which God requires of me), it is not enough to just know that God is trying to tell me something. I must now know exactly what He is saying to me, although He is using the same means (paradigms and patterns) He has used previously, but this time to relay a different message.

A potential danger in experiencing the *When* of Prophetic Paradigms and Patterns is that if we do not learn to distinguish the differences in what God is trying to teach us in a similar *when*, we will become frustrated. It will appear to the unlearned that we are going through the same thing repeatedly, but to no avail. Ironically, it might be that we did not fail the previous *when*, but that there is yet another facet of us that God is wanting to perfect. We then become so focused on "not having to go through this again" until we are not in tune with the specific results that God is trying to achieve. Then, having lost our focus, we really do "botch" the *when*, thus creating the very situation of failure that we were trying to avoid all along (a sort of "that-which-I-hate-that-I-do" [Romans 7:15] situation in reverse). When we learn to identify the paradigms and patterns that God uses to teach us or to get our attention, we save ourselves the grief and misery of having to do the same things over and over again.

Conversely, the joy in successfully completing the *When* of Prophetic Paradigms and Patterns is that of a greater level of spiritual maturity and power. We move from "...glory to glory..." (II Corinthians 3:18) in our understanding of who we are in God and what He wants to accomplish in us and through us. Through this *when*, we gain awareness that every nuance of our being is under the Divine Authority and Supervision of God. This revelation fortifies and energizes us for our prophetic walk in this earth realm.

Scriptural examples of the *When* of Prophetic Paradigms and Patterns include the story of David's calming of Saul's evil spirit. Note that how in the first two scriptures, God used David's singing to calm Saul. However, in the last four verses, David, using the same means (paradigm and pattern) he had previously used, attempted to perform the same task, only to find that it didn't work:

Let our lord now command thy servants, which are before thee, to seek out a man, who is a cunning player on a harp: and it shall come to pass, when the evil spirit from God is upon thee, that he shall play with his hand, and thou shalt be well.
- I Samuel 16:16

And it came to pass, when the evil spirit from God was upon Saul, that David took an harp, and played with his hand: so Saul was refreshed, and was well, and the evil spirit departed from him." – I Samuel 16:23

And it came to pass on the morrow, that the evil spirit from God came upon Saul, and he prophesied in the midst of the house: and David played with his hand, as at other times: and there was a javelin in Saul's hand.

And Saul cast the javelin; for he said, I will smite David even to the wall with it. And David avoided out of his presence twice. – I Samuel 18:10-11

And the evil spirit from the LORD was upon Saul, as he sat in his house with his javelin in his hand; and David played with his hand.

And Saul sought to smite David even to the wall with the javelin: but he slipped away out of Saul's presence, and he smote the javelin into the wall: and David fled, and escaped that night. – I Samuel 19:9-10

5

The When of Abundant Grace and Mercy

ecause the number five symbolizes mercy, it is fitting that this *when* - the *When* of Abundant Grace and Mercy — is Chapter Five. The definition of *when* used here means, "in spite of the fact that: although." For example, we might say, "After being in that car accident, I lived *when* I should have died."

During the *When* of Abundant Grace and Mercy, we come to acknowledge and appreciate the times in our lives when we were deserving of chastisement, but God gave us another chance. It is here that we embrace the fact that *when* we should have died in our sins, God spared our lives and gave us the gift of salvation. *When* we should have given up because we would not trust Him, God gave us the strength to go on. *When* we should have received harsh consequences for acts of disobedience, God levied the hand of the enemy in our lives. And, *when* we should have been exposed for those acts, God covered us and spared us the humiliation and judgment of others. Through His grace and mercy, God kept us, protected us and secured us to be able to go to the next level in Him. All of this occurred during a time in which we are totally undeserving and ungrateful — during our *Whens* of Abundant Grace and Mercy.

Before we can appreciate the *When* of Abundant Grace and Mercy, we must understand what grace and mercy are. The concepts of grace and mercy are often mistakenly used interchangeably. While the concepts of grace and mercy share some similarities, they are actually distinctly different. Admittedly, I have always known that there were differences between grace and mercy, but until I started writing this chapter, I never fully understood exactly what those differences were. Because I did not have an inkling as to how to verbalize these differences, I wondered what I would write about this *when*. In beginning to write this chapter, I prayed to ask God to give me clarity concerning the differences between grace and mercy. He instructed me to research their definitions.

I found that *grace* comes from the Greek word *charis*, which is the word for a divine graciousness that has "influence upon the heart, and its reflection in the life." Charis is the word from which the words *charity* and *character* are derived. It also means "acceptable, benefit, favor." In researching the word *mercy*, I discovered that it comes from the Greek word *elyos*, which means "compassion". Elyos, when used in the scriptures, denotes extremely tender mercy.

From the definitions, I gathered that grace means "benefit and favor". Mercy, on the other hand, means "compassion". These definitions were somewhat helpful. Nevertheless, I still felt like I needed more clarity as to what God wanted me to understand about these concepts. Even after researching the definitions, I still did not feel like I was comfortable enough with the subjects of grace and mercy to be able to write about them. Consequently, I actually postponed the writing of this chapter for months. I started on the chapter after I wrote *Chapter Four*, but drew a blank while writing it. Frustrated, I did not complete this chapter until after I had finished writing the other seven *When* chapters and a large portion of Chapter Nine.

In fact, one night, after writing into the wee hours of the morning, I prayed about omitting this chapter altogether. However, I did not get a release in my spirit to do so. At that point, I lay down and was just about to go to sleep, when God told me to get up and get a pen and some paper. Sensing the urgency of the matter, I rose, - sleepy-eyed and mildly dazed — stumbled out of bed and across the room to my writing corner. As I was regaining my senses, I found my pen and paper. God then told me to write the following:

Grace is –

Goodness
Reflected –
(the) Arisen
Christ
Exemplified.

Then, He said to write this:

Mercy is –

Mistakes/Misdoings
Exonerated/Erased (and)
Rectified;
Compassion
Yielded.

At this point, it was as if the proverbial light bulb popped on in my head. Realizing that there would be no sleep for me that night, I stayed awake —having become instantly refreshed and exhilarated because I was ready to receive the long-awaited revelations about grace and mercy I knew that He was about to give me. As I was certain that He would, He spoke to me and told me to write what I have written in the rest of this chapter.

G.R.A.C.E.

God began teaching me concerning the anagram for grace — *Goodness reflected — (the) Arisen Christ exemplified.* God said that His granting us grace is a process by which

He allows His Goodness to be reflected in our lives. What this means is that when God grants us grace, He (who is Goodness), allows His Divine reflection or countenance to be seen in us. His Goodness outshines all of our imperfections and insecurities so that when people look at us, they do not notice our shortcomings. All they see is Him — Goodness — reflected in us in the area in which God has granted us grace. Because of this, we receive the favor of man, even at times when it would seem that we are grossly undeserving of such favor.

Consequently, when God's Goodness is reflected in us, we take on the countenance of the "Arisen Christ". We begin to exemplify Him in the earth realm. God said that it is important that the distinction is made that we exemplify the *Arisen* Christ, as opposed to *Jesus*. This distinction is necessary because of the differences between the natures of Jesus when He walked the earth versus Jesus the Arisen Christ. Granted, when we speak of Jesus and Jesus the Arisen Christ, we are making reference to the same being — the Divine Son of God, born of a virgin and sent to save the world from sin (Luke 2:11). However, Jesus the Arisen Christ, moved in a greater level of power and authority than before He was crucified and resurrected. In fact, in Matthew 28:18b, Jesus says, *"All power is given unto me in heaven and in earth."* The word *power* used in this verse comes from the Greek word *exousia*, which means "superhuman, authority, jurisdiction."

Therefore, when we receive grace and reflect God's Goodness, we are displaying the *exousia* power of Jesus the Arisen Christ. When He arose, the Arisen Christ went down into hell to set captives free. The Arisen Christ conquered death and the grave (I Corinthians. 15:15). The same Arisen Christ returned to earth and walked among the disciples (Luke 24:15). He returned to heaven in the clouds, vowing to prepare a place for the People of the Lord (Luke 24:51). *Jesus* was *powerful*, but the *Arisen Christ* is *omnipotent*. And, when God grants us grace, this same omnipotence is reflected in us. At that moment, we are His reflection — *we look like Him*. It is no wonder, then, that favor accompanies grace; all who look upon us cannot help but be in awe of the magnificent power that is being reflected by us. When God has granted us grace, even those who do not know Jesus Christ as their savior must reverence Him in us.

Growing in Grace

God gives grace as He so desires. But, we also receive various levels of grace throughout our walk with God, thereby "growing in grace." Growing in grace means that we are mature spiritually and, with each step, are becoming more like God. As we shed our carnality and allow God to "cleanse us of all unrighteousness", we become better "reflectors" of His Goodness. That means that His Grace will be more visible in us. When people look at us, they will see less of our fleshly way of thinking and doing and a clearer picture of the Arisen Christ. I Corinthians 13:12 addresses this point.

> *For now we see through a glass, darkly; but then face to face: now I know in part; but then shall I know even as also I am known.*

This passage begins by discussing seeing through a glass. The glass in this verse comes from the Greek word *esoptron*, which is not a transparent sheet of glass like a window. Instead, an esoptron is a mirror. Paul uses the metaphor of a mirror to describe the process by which he was measuring his spiritual growth and understanding.

He says that at a certain level of grace, we can only see a dim (dark) reflection of the Arisen Christ in us. However, as we grow in grace, we will see the reflection "face to face" or the reflection of Christ within us will be clear. Paul further says that, at the time that he was writing that verse, he only *"knew* [the mysteries of God] *in part"*. However, he said, there would come a time in which he would mature spiritually and, therefore grow in grace. At that point that he would know the mysteries of God "just as sure as he was Paul" (i.e., *"just as I am known"*). By making this statement, Paul is implying that there is a direct correlation between growing in grace and knowing the Word of God and/or receiving Divine Revelation from God. In fact, Peter, too, reiterated this idea of the relationship between grace and knowledge in II Peter 3:18, which says the following:

> But grow in grace, **and** in the knowledge of our Lord and Saviour Jesus Christ. To him be glory both now and for ever. Amen.

God said that the more we learn of His Word, the more grace we are subject to be granted. He said that this is a prophetic principle, which is soundly based upon Biblical principle. God explained it to me in the following manner:

John 1:1 says, *"In the beginning* [....] *the Word was with God and the Word was God."* John 1:14a-b says, *"And the Word was made flesh and dwelt among us."* Therefore, if we learn the Word of God, then we grow in the knowledge of God (because *"the Word was God"* and God does not change [Malachi 3:6]). If Jesus was the Word made flesh, then as we learn the Word of God and grow in the knowledge of God, we are also learning more about Jesus and growing spiritually. When we receive grace, we are reflecting the

Arisen Christ. Therefore, as we read our Bible, hear the word preached and listen to God, we are receiving the Gospel — the good news about the Arisen Christ. In addition, Isaiah 55:11 says, *"[God's] word shall not return unto [Him] void."* So we know then that as we take this Word in, it will in turn perform the work in us that God has ordained; it will change us in some manner so that we have become more like Jesus. Consequently, the more we are changed by the printed, preached and spoken word and by the Living Word (Jesus), the better we can reflect Him in our lives. When we adhere to the Word, we exemplify Him. As a result, our growing in knowledge has caused us to also grow in grace.

The process of growing in knowledge and thereby seeing a clearer reflection of Christ in our lives is depicted in I John 3:2, which says the following:

> *Beloved, now are we the sons of God, and it doth not yet appear what we shall be: but we know that, when he shall appear* [as we grow more in knowledge and grace], *we shall be like him* [because we will have been changed by the Word]; *for we shall see him as he is* [because He will be more clearly reflected in us].

The same thought is stated in a different manner in Romans 6:1-2, which says the following:

> *What shall we say then? Shall we continue in sin, that grace may* abound **[i.e., Can we grow in grace *without* growing in knowledge]**?

> *God forbid* **[No!]**. *How shall we, that are dead to sin, live any longer therein?*

Moving from Glory to Glory

So, as we grow in knowledge, we also grow in grace. However, as we grow in grace, we also *move from glory to glory*. One New Testament definition of the word *glory* comes from the Greek word *doxa*, which is the root word for the word *doxology*.

Doxa denotes a "very apparent glory." It also means "dignity, honor, praise and worship." When we grow in grace, we receive increasing levels of dignity and honor. Both dignity and honor are attributes of God (Revelations 19:1). Consequently, the more we grow in grace, the more dignity and honor we receive and reflect. That means that we are reflecting God more clearly and at a different spiritual level. Having grown in grace and knowledge, we understand that the goodness, honor and dignity that we reflect is not our own. Therefore, we take no credit for them, nor do we take for granted the favor that has been bestowed upon us because of them. In fact, because we have received this spiritual truth, there is something within us that desires to praise and worship God more reverently than ever before.

So, then, as we move from glory to glory, we increase our *"praise and worship"*, so much so until an attitude of praise and worship becomes *"very apparent"* in our lives. Ironically, because we have increased our praise and worship, those looking at us begin to "sing our praises" because they see the power of God working in our life as a result of our growing in grace. At that point, if we are wise, we, in turn, will then give *even more* praise and honor to God for His attributes being manifested in our lives. In doing so, we enter into yet a deeper realm of praise and worship (because we have come to know Him better and can communicate with Him more effectively). This is a continuous cycle in the life of the serious Believer. Each time this cycle occurs, we have *moved from glory to glory*. II Corinthians 3:18 speaks of the process of moving from glory to glory as it relates to growing in grace. It says the following:

> *But we all, with open face beholding as in a glass* [a mirror] *the glory of the Lord, are changed into the same image from glory to glory, even as by the Spirit of the Lord.*

Revisiting our definition of *when* used in this chapter, (i.e., "in spite of the fact that"), we see that God gives us grace "in spite of the fact that" we do not always live in a manner which pleases Him. Nevertheless, He allows us to become closer to Him and, through grace, serve as His Reflections.

M.E.R.C.Y.

We have previously discussed grace. We will now discuss mercy — *Mistakes/Misdoings exonerated (erased) (and) rectified; compassion yielded*. Using the anagram, we see that through mercy, our mistakes are exonerated (or, "cleared from accusation or blame"). Our misdoings — *things we did on purpose, but should not have done* — are erased or "blotted out" from the memory of God (Psalm 51:1) and we are forgiven of our wrong doings. The forgiveness of God is a blessing in and of itself. However, God said that mercy *exceeds* mere forgiveness. In fact, God said that mercy is *compassionate* forgiveness.

God's Soft Spot

The word *compassion* as used in the New Testament comes from the Greek word *splagchnizomai*, which is the root word from which *spleen* is derived. Splagchnizomai means, "to literally yearn from deep within," as if one was yearning from his bowels. It is also defined as "deep, inward affection." Ironically, the Greek word for *bowels* is also a form of splagchnizomai. Likewise, the Old Testament word for *bowels* comes from the Hebrew word *mayaw*, which, not only means the bowels or abdomen area, but encompasses the "soft, inward parts"; specifically, the stomach, the heart, the uterus and other inward reproductive parts. Therefore, when we petition God for mercy and receive it from Him, we have found God's "soft spot"; we have touched the "heart" of God.

Through mercy, God goes beyond forgiving our sins. He grants us compassion and spares us the suffering that we should rightfully experience as the consequences of our actions. This is not to say that mercy alleviates the need for us to pay penance for our sins. To make such a statement would negate the Biblical principle set forth in Galatians 6:7b which says, *"Whatsoever a man soweth, that shall he also reap."* Instead, when God shows us mercy, He is showing leniency in meting out what we reap. In showing mercy, He is taking into account our human frailties and weakness. He understands that we as His children sometimes allow ourselves to "follow after the flesh" instead of doing what we know God has commanded us to do. God still chastises us, but, when we receive His mercy, the chastisement is not nearly as severe as it would have been in the absence of His mercy.

Mercy-based Salvation

The concept of mercy — *compassionate forgiveness* — is an essential factor upon which the premise of salvation is based. God loved us so much and was so compassionate about our redemption until He sent Jesus—His only Begotten Son — to save us from our sins. This Biblical truth is recounted in the widely quoted passage of John 3:16-17, which is as follows:

For God so loved the world, that he gave his only begotten Son, that whosoever believeth in him should not perish, but have everlasting life.

For God sent not his Son into the world to condemn the world; but that the world through him might be saved.

From these verses, we can see both the magnitude and manifestation of God's mercy toward us. Because it was His Desire for those that "believeth in Him" to "not perish", God felt great compassion for us. He literally yearned within His Divine *"bowels"* (i.e., splagchnizomai/mayaw) for us, *in spite of the fact that* mankind had already demonstrated a propensity for unrighteous living. His yearning was manifested as He sent Jesus — the Son sired from God's "bowels" — to serve as a living sacrifice for mankind.

Lord, Have Mercy!

It is unfathomable that we as mortals would ever presume to tell Omnipotent God what to do at any time. This is especially true of trying to *make* God grant us mercy. Romans 9:14-18 clearly states that we cannot, *under any circumstances*, force God to show us mercy. It says the following:

What shall we say then? Is there unrighteousness with God? God forbid.

For he saith to Moses, I will have mercy on whom I will have mercy, and I will have compassion on whom I will have compassion.

So then it is not of him that willeth, nor of him that runneth, but of God that sheweth mercy.

For the scripture saith unto Pharoah, Even for this same purpose have I raised thee up, that I might shew my power in thee, and that my name might be declared throughout all the earth.

Therefore hath he mercy on whom he will have mercy, and whom he will he hardeneth.

God said that while we cannot force Him to be merciful, there are reasons that He chooses to have mercy upon us. One reason that God shows us mercy is because of our sincere repentance. Repentance is necessary before compassionate forgiveness can take place (Mark 1:4). God also shows us mercy when we live godly lives (II Timothy 1:16-18). This is because when we live a godly life and, for some reason, have a need for mercy, God knows that we are well meaning and trustworthy. He knows that if He bestows mercy upon us, we will be restored to our rightful place in the Household of Faith, just as the Prodigal Son received restoration (Luke 15:11-32).

Two other reasons that God grants us mercy are discussed below.

1. **God grants us mercy when we have shown mercy to others.**

Blessed are the merciful, for they shall obtain mercy. **–Matthew 5:7**

Those who show mercy are more apt to understand the value of mercy than those who are unmerciful. When we show mercy to someone who has wronged us or who is undeserving of mercy, we are rendering compassionate forgiveness from our innermost being. We are delving into our spirits; past the fleshly way of thinking, beyond the hurts that person has inflicted upon us. We are resisting the temptation to turn our backs on them, understanding that no matter what they have done to us, vengeance is the Lord's (Deuteronomy 32:35). In sowing compassionate forgiveness into others, we are bestowing mercy upon them. As with grace, we will reap what we sow (Galatians 6:7). Therefore, as we sow mercy, God will have mercy upon us. He will also move on others to show us mercy in our time of need.

Lying Vanities

They that observe lying vanities forsake their own mercy.

But I will sacrifice unto thee with the voice of thanksgiving; I will pay that that I have vowed. Salvation is of the Lord. – Jonah 2:8-9

The story of Jonah being swallowed by "great fish" is a perfect example of what happens when we do not show mercy to others. The story of Jonah begins with God commanding Jonah to go preach to the notoriously sinful Ninevites (1:1-2). Instead of being obedient, unmerciful Jonah chose to run from God and caught a ride on a ship going to Tarshish (1:3). God allowed the ship that Jonah was on to be caught in a storm out on the sea (Jonah 1:4). When Jonah realized what was happening, he urged the others on the ship to throw him overboard. Jonah was thrown overboard and, immediately, the storm subsided (1:14-15). Jonah was then swallowed by a big fish.The second chapter of the Book of Jonah is a prayer Jonah rendered while inside the belly of the great fish. In the above-cited Jonah 2:8-9, Jonah is concluding the prayer/testimony. Going through such an ordeal was a spiritual eye-opener for Jonah. Having been inside the fish for three days, Jonah had time to reflect upon his mistakes. During this time, Jonah received an important revelation.

Jonah learned that an unwillingness to show mercy to others stems from a shortcoming within ourselves. Jonah described this shortcoming as "lying vanities." The word *vanities* used in this instance comes from the Hebrew word *habel*. It means "an emptiness; something transitory and unsatisfactory."

In my ministry and in life experiences, I have learned that people who are extremely judgmental of others are, themselves, extremely insecure. In fact, judgmental people often use their disdain and disapproval of others to cover up the fact that they are not happy with a part of themselves. This is because while they seem to have everything going for them on the outside, on the inside there is a *habel* — *"an emptiness; something transitory [unstable] and unsatisfactory."* Throughout the years, these tormented souls have learned to mask this area by constantly pointing the finger at other people. They do so because they are, in fact, deceived.

The deception occurs because the emptiness — *the vanity* — has been "manufactured" and assigned to them by the enemy. Its purpose is to deceive them by telling them only what they want to hear (which may not always be the truth). Therefore, because they do not want to deal with painful, unflattering areas of their own lives, the vanity only speaks to them about the shortcomings of others, even magnifying the faults of others in the minds of judgmental people. While in the belly of the fish, Jonah recognized the deception that had taken place and described the occurrence as a *lying* vanity. Therefore, when judgmental people "observe lying vanities, they can only recognize and dwell on the shortcomings of others but cannot admit to their own faults. At this point, not only are they judgmental, but they have now become unmerciful. They feel as if they cannot afford to show others mercy and forgive them because, in truth, unmerciful people have not forgiven themselves for many things. Because they will not show mercy, they will not receive mercy. This is a biblical principle stated in Matthew 7:2, which says, *"For with what judgment yet judge, ye shall be judged: and with what measure ye mete, it shall be measured to you again."* Therefore, as Jonah learned, in observing lying vanities, unmerciful people forsake their own mercy.

God said that there are many of us within the Body of Christ who observe lying vanities. I prophesy to you by the unction of the Holy Ghost that if we as a Body are to grow and become the manifested Church of the Most High God, we can no longer observe lying vanities. God said the He wants to show us mercy — *He wants to forgive us and bring us into right standing with Him.* But, because we have chosen not to show mercy to others, He will not grant us mercy in the condition that we are in. He said that we are too quick to point the finger at each other, tearing each other down and harping on the shortcomings of our Brothers and Sisters. Many a soul has been lost because of our judgmental and unmerciful behavior; there have been those who once walked with God, but turned away because of the unrelenting scrutiny of the so-called People of the Lord. The very ministers and elders of the Gospel to which they turned for advice and spiritual guidance shunned them and made them feel unwelcome in the Household of Faith. God said that a day of reckoning is shortly coming and those who would not show mercy to others must give an account of their deeds. God said that if we will not show mercy now, that He will not show us mercy on that day of reckoning.

2. **God has mercy upon us when we have sinned unwillingly and/or unknowingly, but have since repented.**

And I thank Christ Jesus our Lord, who hath enabled me, for that he counted me faithful, putting me into the ministry;

Who was before a blasphemer, and a persecutor, and injurious: **but I obtained mercy, because I did it ignorantly in unbelief.** *– I Timothy 1:12-13*

Paul, who refers to himself as the chief of sinners (I Timothy 1:15), wrote the above scriptures as part of a letter to Timothy. He begins verse 12 by giving thanks to "Christ Jesus" for calling and ordaining him to serve in ministry. Paul said goes on to say that he was called for ministry *in spite of the fact that* in times past, he persecuted Christians. Nevertheless, Paul said, God used him for the spreading of the Gospel. He said that the reason that he was shown so much compassion was because during the time when he was not saved and was "a blasphemer, a persecutor and injurious", he "obtained mercy" from God. Paul stated that God granted him this mercy because at the time of his wrongdoing, Paul acted "ignorantly in unbelief."

Paul's usage of the phrase *"ignorantly in unbelief"* was not happenstance. Paul realized that there is a difference in merely sinning because of ignorance versus sinning because of ignorance generated by unbelief. Before he was saved, Paul's job was to make life as miserable for Christians as he possibly could. He even killed or orchestrated the deaths of many men of God. One could argue that, even without knowing God, Paul had to know, on some moral level, that killing is wrong (no matter who is being killed).

However, Paul was led by a sense of duty and responsibility to his profession. He was operating by the laws of the land. In persecuting Christians before he got saved, Paul was "just doing his job." Because he did not realize the gravity of what he was doing, Paul was operating in *ignorance*. That is, in ignorance, he truly did not know that what he was doing was wrong based on God's laws. This is because Paul had not yet come to know Christ Jesus as his personal savior. Until his Damascus Road experience (Acts 9), Paul had never experienced feelings of conviction about killing Christians. He had never had a reason to *have to* adhere to the Word of God. So, not only did he act in ignorance, but he also operated in *unbelief*, which means that Paul did not yet possess a strong God-consciousness. He neither believed that he was wrong nor that there were Divinely mandated consequences for his actions. However, once Paul came into the knowledge of God, accepted Jesus as His personal savior and began to do the work of the ministry, he sincerely repented for persecuting the Christians. At that point, God granted him mercy.

God said that He does *not necessarily grant mercy just because we have sinned ignorantly*, as many Christians have been taught. I, myself, had been taught to believe this. When I asked God how to illustrate this point, He reminded me of the following incident:

A few years ago, I was serving as an altar worker, ministering to a woman at the altar. God had directed me to explain a biblical truth to her that He had previously revealed to me. The teaching was on a subject with which the woman had been struggling; it concerned an area in her life that God wanted her to change. She would go to the altar — Sunday after Sunday — wailing and crying, begging God to "give her another chance" to overcome this problem. However, although *it seemed* as if the woman was sincerely praying to God to give her an answer, she did not want to change or do what it took to rectify the problem. Like many of us, she did not *really* want help; *she just wanted to talk about it.* I told her that God had spoken a specific Prophetic Word to me concerning her situation. As I began to relay that Word to her, she interrupted me, saying, "Don't tell me, 'cause I don't want to know that right now. The Bible says that I am not accountable for anything that I don't know. So, if I don't know, I don't have to do it!" Flabbergasted, I went on to minister to someone else. I left her standing there, sniffling and still "repenting".

God said that the Body of Christ has claimed and feigned ignorance for too long. We use ignorance as an excuse for not correcting problems or for not doing what we know is the right thing. It is one thing if we have not received teaching on a certain matter or if we need spiritual clarity or leadership. But, when we are ignorant and choose to remain so, God is not as apt to show us mercy.

GRACE AND MERCY

It is important to understand that while grace and mercy are distinctly different, they actually work hand in hand. That is, there can be no grace without mercy. Conversely, there can be no mercy without grace. The story of Jonah supports these two statements and provides other revelations regarding the relationship between grace and mercy.

No Mercy Without Grace

In revisiting the story of Jonah, we recall that a "great fish" had swallowed Jonah. The word *fish* in this verse comes from the Hebrew word *dawg*. It means, "squirming (like a fish's tail), timid and prolific." As we said earlier, the Book of Jonah begins with God giving Jonah a Divine Call to go minister to the people at Ninevah (1:1-2). Romans 8:30 b-c declares that "*...whom he [God] called, them he also justified, and whom we justified, them he also glorified*". The word *glorified* used in this verse comes from the Greek word *doxazo* — *the same root word from which grace is derived.* Doxazo means "to render (or esteem) glorious; to make full of honor; to magnify." So, when God calls us, He not only *justifies* us, but He *magnifies (glorifies)* us. The glorification does not occur because we have suddenly become super spiritual or all-righteous. Instead, the glorification occurs because God has revealed more of Himself in us; He has given us more grace to minister in that area.

Therefore, when God called Jonah, He also gave him the grace to minister to the people of Ninevah. But, when Jonah disobeyed God and boarded the ship headed for Tarshish, God was displeased with Jonah's actions. At that point, Jonah did not use the grace God had bestowed upon him for its appointed purpose. As such, at the moment of his disobedience, *Jonah fell from grace.* That is, in not going to the appointed place at the appointed time, Jonah had removed himself from the place of spiritual oneness with God; the place in which God could be "reflected" in his life. Jonah's "falling" into the water — his being thrown overboard and swallowed by the great fish — was merely *a physical manifestation* of *what had already taken place in the spirit realm.* For the *"three days and three nights"* (Jonah 1:17) that Jonah was in the belly of the great fish, Jonah was without God's grace.

God said that when we fall from grace, He prepares a "great fish" (*dawg*) for each of us. Therefore, when we fall from grace, we *"go to the dawgs"*. We are "swallowed up" in a mess of our own making. It is a dark, lonely place in which all we can do is sit and think about where we went wrong. There is Word (water) all around us, but we cannot receive it. Moreover, even if we could, it is too deep for us to "rightly divide" (to swim in or to navigate through). This is mostly because, in the absence of grace, we are not "equipped" to handle it. Like the definition of the great fish, having fallen from grace makes us "squirm". We have been caught in our wrongdoing and are now paying the price for it. This makes us extremely uncomfortable and, just as Jonah, we begin to cry out to God to have mercy on us.

As we studied earlier, Jonah received the revelation concerning lying vanities and prayed a prayer of repentance (Jonah 2:8-9). After having been in the belly of the great fish for "three days and three nights", it seemed as if Jonah had learned the error of his ways. As he prayed, Jonah touched the heart of God. God showed him mercy and caused the great fish to vomit Jonah out on dry land (Jonah 2:10). Although Jonah prayed to God inside the belly of the fish, God did not speak to Jonah again until Jonah was out of the fish's belly and on dry land. Ironically, after Jonah's horrible ordeal, God did not speak words of encouragement or sympathy. Instead, the first words God spoke to Him were those repeating the calling to Jonah to do what He had directed Jonah to do in the first place — to go preach to the people of Ninevah (Jonah 3:1-2). Jonah was exonerated and re-released to do what God told him to do in the first place. God knew that when Jonah prayed inside the fish, he was sincere.

Therefore, *at the exact moment that Jonah prayed inside the great fish — before God audibly spoke to Jonah — God again gave Him grace to go and preach.* He did so because Jonah showed he was desirous of doing what God said. God's re-calling him on an audible (physical) level only confirmed what had already taken place in the spirit realm. That is, *after* God gave Jonah *grace*, He then bestowed *mercy* upon him. From that experience, Jonah learned that *there can be no true mercy without our first receiving true grace.*

No Grace without Mercy

Just as there can be no grace without mercy, there can also be no mercy without grace. This is evident in the latter part of the story of Jonah. After being released from the fish's belly and re-receiving the call to preach to the Ninevites, Jonah embarks upon a three-day journey to Nineveh. Upon arriving in Ninevah, Jonah preached to the Ninevites, saying that the Lord commanded them to repent from their evil ways. The Ninevites took heed to what God said through Jonah and fasted and repented (3:5). As a result of their obedience, God showed them mercy and forgave them of the sins. In doing so, the Ninevites were spared the vengeance and destruction that would have ensued had they not taken heed to God's Word. God's leniency toward them made Jonah extremely upset (4:1). Jonah did not think the Ninevites deserved such mercy because their history as a disobedient people, whose founder's name — Nimrod — even means, *"rebel"* (Genesis 10:8-10).

At the beginning of his journey, Jonah felt justified in running from assignment to preach to the Ninevites based on what he knew about their history. That is, he assumed that there was no hope for them, so why bother to go preach to them. Then, after having been released from the fish's belly, apparently, he still did not believe that the Ninevites were going to change. In fact, the story seems to suggest that Jonah went to preach to the Ninevites in the expectation that they *would not* heed the Word of the Lord and would, therefore, be punished severely. But, when this did not happen, Jonah became angry. In fact, Jonah became so angry until he petitioned God to let him die (4:2-3). God, yet being merciful, tried to reason with Jonah, asking him, *"Doest thou well to be angry? (4:4)"* Jonah, frustrated and wroth, ignored God and did not respond to God's question. Instead, Jonah went to the east side of the city to sit and sulk. He set up a booth to have some shade in which he could sit and watch the Ninevites (4:5). Once again, Jonah had allowed his unmerciful and judgmental nature to move him to a place outside of the will of God.

The word *booth* used in Jonah 4:5 comes from the Hebrew word *cukkah*. In addition to denoting a booth, it also means "lair, covert, den, pavilion, tabernacle and tent." Jonah made this booth to shield him from the sun and the elements as he sat and angrily watched the Ninevites. However, God knew that the booth would not provide adequate shade, so He *"prepared a gourd, and made it to come up over Jonah, that it might be a shadow over his head, to deliver him from grief"* (4:6). Jonah was pleased with the shade that the gourd provided. The word *gourd* used here comes from the Hebrew word *qiyqayown*. Ironically, *qiyqayown* comes from the root word *qayah — the Hebrew word for vomit*. The act of vomiting denotes a purging and humiliation.

Just as God had prepared the gourd, God also prepared a worm to come and smite the gourd (4:6). The gourd withered and Jonah was left with inadequate protection from the elements. Next, God sent a "vehement east wind" to blow on Jonah. The wind blew with such great force and with such heat until it literally caused Jonah to faint. Once again, Jonah wished for death (4:8).

In building the booth to view the Ninevites, Jonah, in his anger did not realize that while he could see the Ninevites, the Ninevites could also see him! However, the Ninevites did not look upon Jonah with the same disdain and loathing that Jonah had toward them. Having received the Word of God through Jonah, the Ninevites viewed Jonah as a Man of God who had been sent to save them from utter destruction. They saw and relished the call of God upon his life; they recognized the grace of God upon Jonah. However, unmerciful and judgmental Jonah was bent on the destruction of the Ninevites. Angry with God, Jonah decided that he could "cover" himself and, therefore, prepared the booth. God had to show Jonah the error of his ways, so in addition to Jonah's inadequate shelter — *the booth* — God prepared the gourd. That is, just like with the great fish, God allowed Jonah to "*return to his own vomit*". With the gourd, Jonah was shielded from the heat and wind because God was covering him. Through the gourd, God was showing Jonah what true mercy was. However, when God allowed the worm to destroy the gourd, God was also taking away His *mercy*. Jonah discovered that the booth — *his own covering, his own mercy* — would not sufficiently protect him. The heat became so intense until Jonah fainted and wished for death. There lay Jonah — the Man of God who had just preached such a powerful, life-changing word to the Ninevites — weak and exposed for God and all the Ninevites to see, wishing for death. At that point in Jonah's life, *there was no grace* (no covering of the Lord; no reflection of God in his life) *because there was no mercy.*

God said that once He grants us grace, we must be careful not to erect *spiritual booths* (i.e., pavilions, tabernacles, tents), in our lives. For, within our own "tabernacles", we worship *ourselves* — the creators and gods of our tabernacles. When we are in such spiritual places, we have no regard for what God would say to us. Also, when we receive grace, we must remember that we are mere humans and as much as we may "reflect" God, we are NOT God. As such, although we may be able to justify our actions to ourselves and thereby make ourselves feel better, *we cannot "cover" ourselves*. God must be our covering (our Protection). He alone can bestow mercy and, yes, we desperately need the mercies of God. We are never so righteous as to not to need Him. Consequently, when we begin to think that we are without need of mercy or that we are more deserving of it than others are, God will allow circumstances to occur which become "too hot for us to handle". At that point, not only do we lose the mercy of God, but we also are no longer operating under His grace. If we are wise, we realize that we "can't stand the heat" and re-align ourselves with the Word of God and His Will for our lives. We then have an "attitude adjustment" and accept whatever God has said.

6

The When of Alternative Means

he next definition of *when* we will discuss is the one that means, "considering that". As an example of its use, we might say, "Why wait until lunch to eat *when* breakfast has been prepared?" This *when* is the *When* of Alternative Means. During this *when*, God shows us that He uses specific means to accomplish specific tasks in our lives. During this *when* we also learn that God sometimes uses alternative means to achieve the same overall purpose. In illustrating this principle to me, God illuminated some prophetic revelations regarding what He called *Spiritual Mathematics*. He said that in order for us to fully comprehend the *When* of Alternative Means, we must first understand the concepts of spiritual counting, addition, subtraction, multiplication and division. Each of these processes brings with it a season that we will experience in our lives.

SPIRITUAL COUNTING

Before we can perform any type of mathematical process, we must first learn to count. Defined, *counting* is "to indicate or name by units or groups to find the total number of units involved". Another definition of counting is "to name the numbers up to and including (i.e., counting to ten)." Because of the lifelong importance of proper counting, it is one of the first skills we learn as children. When we are very young, the counting process is engrained in us to the extent that we can recognize, write and even recite numbers by rote memorization.

At its basest level, counting is done sequentially and on a unit-by-unit basis (e.g., if we were counting baskets, we would count, "one basket, two baskets, three baskets", etc.) As we become more skilled in counting, we can then "graduate" to counting in multiples (i.e., counting by twos, counting by fives, etc.).

Count is also defined as "to depend" (*e.g., We can count on God.*). Other definitions of *count* are "to take something into consideration" and "to esteem or establish". A biblical example of these definitions is found in James 1:2-3, which reads:

My brethren, count it all joy when ye fall into divers temptations;

Knowing this, that they trying of your faith worketh patience.

God said that the first step to understanding the *When* of Prophetic Alternatives is *learning to count.* In fact, He said, we go through seasons of counting. During these times, God teaches us to recognize and appreciate our blessings. He also teaches us to remember and count on (depend on) the promises that He has made us. These promises are both those that are in the Bible or those that He spoke to us individually. These blessings and promises will then serve as the spiritual foundation upon which God will then perform other feats in our lives. Just like children learning to count, it is necessary for us literally to commit those blessings and promises to memory, so that, when we are being tested, we can recite them. In doing so, we will be speaking the word of God over our lives for that particular situation. Once we know how to "count", we can then be thankful for what we have and hopeful for what we know He has spoken for us.

Just as with numeric counting, when we learn to count spiritually, we must begin with a simple counting sequence (i.e., 1,2,3, etc.). That is, *God will impart simple biblical truths, principles and promises into our spirits.*

For example, let us *suppose* that, when we got saved, it was prophesied that we would have a world-renown ministry. As our scenario begins, we are in the early stages of salvation. We feel the call of ministry upon our lives, but, because we are young in ministry and have not been taught, we do not see any avenues through which we can minister. Just as during the *When* of Prophetic Inquiry (*Chapter One*), we ask God "*when* will my ministry come to fruition?" If we are not reassured by God at this point in our spiritual walk and our ministry, this type of uncertainty could cause seeds of doubt and frustration to be planted in our spirits. In our scenario, we pray to God and ask him to give us a word concerning this situation. He answers, directing us to read Proverbs 18:16, which says:

> A man's gift maketh room for him, and bringeth him before great men.

This simple, concise Word was just the confirmation we needed from God for that season of our lives. In this scripture, God has confirmed that He has given us a gift. He is also letting us know that, in His due season, that gift will generate an outlet for us to serve in ministry.

Continuing our scenario, time has passed, our gift has indeed made room for us, and we are now embarking upon ministry. However, as with most ministries, we are now experiencing opposition from the enemy as he uses those who do not want to see us prosper. Specifically, it has been alleged that we were never called to ministry in the first place. Again, wanting to know the mind of God concerning this ordeal, we ask God to give us a Prophetic Word concerning our circumstances. During this time of our spiritual life, as we mature in counting and in our walk with God, God begins to speak to us in a more complex manner. Our counting then becomes more advanced (i.e., counting by twos). At this stage, He "takes up where He left off" before and gives continuations of His blessings and promises by leading us to read the following passage of scripture:

And we know that all things work together for good to them that love God, to them who are the called according to his purpose.

For whom he did foreknow, he also did predestinate to be conformed to the image of the Son, that he might be the firstborn among many brethren.

Moreover whom he did predestinate, them he also called: and whom he called, them he also justified: and whom he justified, them he also glorified.

What say we then to these things? If God be for us, who can be against us? **– Psalm 8:28-31**

As we said, we began with the prophesy of ministry. When then received the confirmation of the calling. God built upon these principles and, in the passage above now assures us that, even in the opposition, all things are working together for our good (verse 28). He also gave us spiritual revelation concerning our calling, our justification and our glorification (verses 29 thru 31). He concluded by telling us that yes, He is with us, and with that being the case, no one else's negative opinion of us can harm us. We learn not only to consider God's love for us, but to be thankful for Him loving us so much that He called us, justified us and glorified us for the work of the ministry. In grasping this truth, we have learned to count at this level.

Finally, more years have passed in our scenario and our ministry has grown and has become well established. We have become mature in ministry and in our walk with the Lord. We have developed an intimate relationship with Him and commune with Him on a daily basis. Just as the prophesy stated, God has now opened doors for us to minister internationally. At this point, He has given us great favor so that we are now being invited to speak to people of great wealth, prominence and influence throughout the world. However, although the promise is being fulfilled, the enemy rears his ugly head just as in times past. This time, people with whom we once closely walked have now turned away from us because they are envious of our success or because they do not understand the scope of what God has called us to do. Additionally, we feel that we are often misunderstood and begin to question if, even after achieving the promise of God for our lives, we are really making a difference. *"In fact,"* we ask God, *"why am I in ministry in the first place?"*

We have the promise of ministry through the prophecy. We have the assurance of our gifting and call to ministry. We even have the confirmation that we were called and that God is with us. Yes, we understand all of this, but it is not enough. That is, we now desire a "fresh" word from God. We are hungering for some sort of confirmation for this level; some answer as to the question *"Why am I in ministry in the first place?"* God now teaches us to count at a yet a more advanced level (i.e., counting by 10s or 100s), as He answers our question by simply saying:

"Jesus wept." (John 11:35)

By this point in our walk with God, we have learned that one of the ironies of God is that sometimes the simpler the Word sounds, the more complex it is (e.g., *when*). On the surface, the response "Jesus wept" seems to be an inappropriate, almost nonsensical answer to the question, *"Why am I in ministry in the first place?"* But because we are mature in ministry and in the ways of God, we understand perfectly what God is saying to us. From these two words — *Jesus wept*— we receive the revelation that *we are in ministry to tell others about Jesus,* One who gave the ultimate sacrifice for ministry. That is, we understand that Jesus cared so much about the salvation of mankind that He was willingly crucified for us. We further understand that, when Jesus wept, His weeping was a result of the effect that mankind's sinful nature had upon Him. As His appointed crucifixion time came near, Jesus was saddened that people still did not recognize who He was nor the dire need for salvation. He wept because He loved us. Likewise, we also understand that, in answer to our question, God is saying we are not in ministry of our own accord, but because He has called us to tell His people about Jesus and His ministry of salvation. We can then "count our blessings" and become thankful for the prophesy, the gifting, the calling and the confirmation of the call to ministry upon our lives.

SPIRITUAL ADDITION

In school, after we learn to count, the first mathematical process we study is addition. To add means "to combine (numbers) in a simple quantity or number". After having been drilled with the rote memorization of counting (again, one basket, two baskets, three baskets), we then learn rudimentary addition tables (1+0=1, 1+1=2, 1+2=3, etc.) so that 1 basket +0 baskets = 1 basket and so on). In an addition equation, each part of the problem has a specific name. For instance, in the problem 2+4=6, the 2 is called the *addend*, or the part that will be added to something else. The 4 is the *addendum*, or the thing that is being added. The 6 is called the *sum*, or the result of what has been added. When more than two numbers are added in a single problem (e.g., 1+2+3=6), the first number to be added (1 in this example) is still called the *addend*. The other numbers being added to the first (2 and 3) are *addendums*. The result (6) would still be called the *sum*.

God said that we will experience seasons of spiritual addition. He said these times can best be described as a "give-us-this-day-our-daily-bread" types of seasons in which we pray for something (*sum*) and can literally see God provide each individual part (*addends and addendums*) to answer that specific prayer. For example, during a season of spiritual addition we might pray, "Lord, I have enough money for food this month, but I thank you for enough money to cover the rest of this month's bills." So, in answering our prayer, God takes into account that, based on our prayer, we have all the money we desire for groceries (*addend*). He then provides money to pay rent (*addendum 1*), (+) enough money to pay utilities (*addendum 2*), (+) enough money to pay the car note (*addendum 3*), plus any other monthly expenses. He provides what we requested — enough money to pay that month's bills (*sum*). During seasons of spiritual addition, we can see God work "*precept upon precept; line upon line*" (Isaiah 28:10).

SPIRITUAL SUBTRACTION

The word *subtract* means "to take away by deduction". It comes from the Latin word *subtrahere*, which means "to draw from beneath; withdraw". As with addition, each part of a subtraction problem is given a specific name. For instance, in the equation 6-4=2, the 6 is called the *minuend*, or the number from which the subtracting is done. The 4 is called the *subtrahend*, or the number that is being subtracted. The 2 is called the *difference*, or the outcome of the subtraction process.

God said that there will be seasons of spiritual subtraction in our lives. During these times, God will take things away from various areas of our lives, thus making those areas *spiritual minuends*. During these seasons, the things He takes away (*spiritual subtrahends*) might be habits, relationships, possessions, attitudes or anything else that God chooses to remove from us. He said that once we allow Him to do this work in us, we will be able to see and appreciate the "*difference*" (or the outcome) this season of subtraction will have made in our lives. Due to the subtraction, we will have shed something that prohibited us from achieving His Divine Purpose for our lives.

David's poignant prayer in Psalm 51 is an example of spiritual subtraction. In this passage of scripture, David asks God to remove anything about his life that displeased God. Some verses from this passage are as follows:

> *Purge me with hyssop, and I shall be clean: wash me, and I shall be whiter than snow."*– **verse 7**

> *Hide thy face from my sins, and blot out all mine iniquities.* – **verse 9**

David understood that, as a result of God subtracting these things from his life, there would be a great "difference" in the flowing of the anointing in his life, so much so that he could then minister more effectively:

Then [as a result of the subtraction] will I teach transgressors thy ways; and sinners shall be converted unto thee. – Psalm 51:13

It is also interesting to note that in this passage of scripture while David is imploring God to "take away" many negative things, David also pleads with God to never "subtract" Himself from his life:

Cast me not away from thy presence; and take not thy holy spirit from me. – Psalm 51:11

SPIRITUAL MULTIPLICATION

To multiply means, "to increase in number especially greatly in multiples (to augment)". Multiply also means "to become greater in number, to spread, breed or propagate — to increase". Mathematically speaking, multiplication is the process by which two or more numbers are increased in multiples of each other. In the equation 5x8=40, both 5 and 8 are called *factors*, or numbers which will be multiplied together. However, in addition to being factors, each of them has a specific name. The 5 is called a *multiplicand*, or the number that is to be multiplied by another. The 8 is called the *multiplier*, or the number by which something is being multiplied. 40 is called the *product*, or the result of the multiplication. Our example equation states that it takes eight sets of 5 to equal 40.

The principles of multiplication are derived from addition. In fact, the sum derived by adding the correct amounts of units could equal the product resulting from multiplying. For instance, using the equation above, we see that when we multiply 5 and 8, the product is 40. Using the principle that it takes eight 5's to equal 40, we could use addition to come to the same conclusion, thus creating the equation 5+5+5+5+5+5+5+5=40. However, although addition may be used to yield the same result, multiplication is less time consuming and more efficient.

God said that during a season of spiritual multiplication, He allows areas of our lives to be increased exponentially. He said that during such seasons, He uses multiplication instead of addition to ensure that what He wants us to do or grasp will occur in a shorter amount of time. Sometimes God chooses to multiply our finances, our ministry, or favor, etc. But, at other times, God allows our pain, sorrow, disappointment and other areas of discomfort to be multiplied. God said that even when this occurs, we, as Prophetic People, must be so in tuned with Him until we do not allow ourselves to become alarmed or disillusioned. Instead, He said, we must be assured that He is performing a perfect work, using the right *"factors"* to yield His desired *"product."* During a season of multiplication, we come to know God as El Shaddai, "The God that is More than Enough."

SPIRITUAL DIVISION

Lastly, there is division, which comes from the word *divide*. One definition of divide means "to separate into two or more parts, areas or groups (to distribute or separate)". Another definition is "to possess, enjoy or make use of in common".

In mathematics, division is considered an opposite process of multiplication. This is because while multiplication combines factors to yield a product, division is a de-factoring process by which a number is "broken down". To understand this, let us revisit the equation 5x8=40. In multiplication, we said that factors 5 and 8 multiplied to yield a product of 40. Division, however, reverses that process. For division, we will use the equation 40 ÷ 5 = 8, where 40, which was previously called a product in multiplication, is now called a *dividend* or the number being divided. 5 is now called a *divisor*, or the number by which something is being divided. 8 is now called the *quotient*, or the result. What the division equation says is that 40 can be separated into eight multiples of 5.

For people who have memorized basic multiplication and division tables (i.e., 1x1=1, 2÷2=1, etc.), the equation 40÷5=8 can be solved mentally and with no written calculations. However, in viewing this problem solved by long division methods, we see that there is more than one step to solving this problem:

$$
\begin{array}{r}
8 \text{ r}0 \\
5 \overline{\smash{)}\ 40} \\
-\underline{40} \\
0
\end{array}
$$

To solve this problem, it was determined that 8 is the highest possible number of times that 5 could "go into" 40. 5 was then multiplied by 8, which gave a product of 40. The product of 40 (bottom/second 40) was then subtracted from the dividend of 40 (first/top). This left a difference or remainder (r) of zero. By this process, both 8 and 5 were determined to be factors of 40 because when multiplied they "make up" 40.

God revealed to me that we, His Prophetic People, also experience seasons of spiritual division. God said that these are times of testing. Ironically, spiritual division often occurs after we have been "multiplied" and are seemingly "on top of the world." After we have been multiplied, we sometimes have the tendency to become smug and comfortable with our newly acquired blessing when, suddenly, it seems that God begins to undo the very multiplication He just completed — *He begins to divide.* That is, He allows us to go through a process by which He shows us "what we are made of." He "breaks us down" and shows us the *"factors"* (i.e., motives and attitudes, for instance) that influence our decisions, desires and actions in the area in which we are being tested. He then seems to subtract the product that He just gave us.

The story of Abraham and Isaac is a prime example of spiritual division (Genesis 22). Abraham, who loved God and had unwavering faith, received the promise that he would father many nations. He also received a promise that he and his wife Sarah would give birth to a son through whom these nations would come (Genesis 15:19). Isaac, the son in whom the promise would begin to be fulfilled, was not born until both Abraham and Sarah were very old. As time went on and Isaac became older, it seemed as God's promise to Abraham was about to be fulfilled, God tells Abraham to literally "divide" his blessing by commanding him to sacrifice Isaac. Abraham, motivated first by his love for God (*spiritual divisor*) takes Isaac (*product/dividend/blessing*) to the appointed place and prepared to sacrifice (*divide*) him.

As Abraham and Isaac approached the altar, Isaac — unaware that he was to be sacrificed — asked, *"Behold the fire and the wood: but where is the lamb for a burnt offering?"* (verse 7) Abraham, knowing that God had commanded him to sacrifice Isaac, responded by saying *"My son, God will provide himself a lamb for a burnt offering."* (verse 8). At that moment, Abraham was talking to Isaac. But, by rendering that faith-based response he also gave God the "right answer" (i.e., the appropriate factor—*the spiritual quotient*) to "solve the problem". Abraham's great faith (*quotient*), when multiplied by his great love for God (*divisor*) yielded the right conditions under which God could trust him with the promises of Isaac and the fathering of many nations. Just as Abraham had spoken,

God sent a ram to be sacrificed, thus allowing Isaac to be spared.

Determining the Means

In relating spiritual mathematics to the *When* of Alternative Means, we can see that God always has more than one way of achieving the same end result. God said that during the *When* of Alternative Means, we as Prophetic People must become sensitive to what He is doing and how He is doing it. This *when* is one which is experienced by all Believers, but it can only be discerned by those whose spiritual perception is keen enough to grasp the concepts of spiritual mathematics. God also said that we learned to detect "repetition" during the *When* of Prophetic Paradigms and Patterns (*Chapter Four*). But, during the *When* of Alternative Means, we now learn that while we can *detect* His pattern once it has been set into motion in our lives, we cannot *predict* the manner in which He will move. But, we can say with absolute certainty that however He chooses to move will glorify Him and will bring to pass the promises He has made us.

For instance, let us suppose that God promised us that we would be multi-millionaires. Yet, we have had a history of job loss and financial troubles. Recently, however, God blessed us with a job in which we were making great money and it seemed as if His promise of wealth was about to come into fruition. Then, unexpectedly we lost this job (or, harder still, God tells us to resign from this job). We are now seemingly worse off financially than ever before, with little to no prospects of obtaining a new job.

Let us further suppose that, in times past, we would pray and God would *"add"* to us by giving us another job that met our immediate financial needs. But now in our scenario, we have entered into a *When* of Prophetic

Alternative Means. Now, God teaches us that the fact that we are unemployed and struggling financially does not necessarily mean that He wants to give us a job. That is, in this season, He may not want to merely *"add"* to us anymore. Instead, He may want us to use this time off work to *count* our blessings and be thankful for what we have and for what He has promised us. This attitude of thankfulness might make us better praisers and worshippers. As we praise and worship and become more in tune with Him, He will equip us spiritually to receive and maintain the promise of great wealth.

Or, perhaps God has sent this season of unemployment to *"subtract"* the distractions of a 9-to-5 job. Maybe He wants us to be still so that He can speak to us concerning His Plan for a multimillion-dollar corporation that He wants to give us.

However, He may want to *"multiply"* us during this season by miraculously releasing the funds, the building and all the necessary resources to get the multimillion-dollar corporation underway.

Finally, perhaps God has placed us in a *"division"* mode, where He is testing our reaction to being unemployed (again) and suffering economic hardship: Will we "pout?" Will we lose faith in the promise that He made to us? Why did we really want to become millionaires in the first place (i.e., what would we do with the money if we had it)? In this place of division, once we prove that our motives are pure and God sees that we are faithful, in His appointed time, He will manifest His promise to us.

7

The When of Prophetic Conditions and Mandates

Our seventh definition of *when* means "in the event that: IF". An example of its usage is the following sentence: He may obtain his license *when* he successfully passes the course. This *when* is called the *When* of Prophetic Conditions and Mandates. During this season of our lives, God gives us prophetic edicts and instructions, of both things to do and things not to do. He also gives us specific revelation concerning the consequences of our actions.

IF-THEN STATEMENTS

In our example sentence, "He may obtain his license when he successfully passes the course," the sentence implies at least two points. First, it states that if the person is successful in passing the course, he may obtain his license. Secondly, it implies that if the person does not pass the course, his license will not be obtained at that time. So then, it is an obvious conclusion that the obtaining of the license is predicated upon passing the course. Another way of stating this would be the following sentence: "If he passes the course, then he may obtain his license." In mathematics, such a statement is called an *"if-then" statement*. An "if-then" statement is considered to be a "two-part" statement that is separated by a comma (,). That is, in our statement, "If he passes the course, then he may obtain his license", is actually two conditional statements joined together to express a logical truth. In solving mathematical/logic "if-then" problems, the statements are considered conditional. This is because the premise of an "if-then" statement is that this two-part statement (i.e., the *"if"* part and the *"then"* part) is only a true statement if both of the parts are true. It is sometimes found that one of the parts is not true, thus making the whole statement false.

It is also possible to have more than one condition (compound conditions) to be met within an "if-then" statement. For instance, we might say, "*If* he attends class regularly *and* passes the course, *then* he will obtain his license." In this instance, we are saying that the conditions of obtaining the license have now been amended to both *attending class* and *passing the course.* In our example in this paragraph, although the person may pass the course, if he does not attend class regularly, he will not obtain the license.

Because of the construction of the English language, the word *then* is sometimes considered redundant and unnecessary to relay the thought of the sentence. For instance, in our example "if-then" statement, we could say, "*If* he passes the course, he may obtain his license." In this instance, neither the use nor the omission of the word *then* would change the meaning of the sentence. Consequently, the sentence would still be considered an "if-then" statement.

God said that during the *When* of Prophetic Conditions and Mandates, He gives us spiritual "if-then" statements. In these statements, He tells us that certain conditions must be met to receive certain results. Likewise, He gives specific conditions and mandates to which we must adhere to both receive certain blessings and to avoid certain consequences.

But, God said, because He cannot lie, there will never be a time when any statement that He makes to us is false. If

He tells us to do something, we must do it or suffer the consequences. He further revealed that because "to whom much is given, much is required" (Luke 12:48), He will sometimes give us "compound conditions" (more than one thing to do at a time). When compound conditions are given, all of conditions must be met to receive the desired outcome.

God said that this *when* is, of sorts, an extension of the *When* of Prophetic Precision and Timing (*Chapter Three*) in which we learned to hear Him and obey instantly. But, He said, in the *When* of Prophetic Conditions and Mandates, not only do we understand that we must do what He said in the manner in which He said. Now, during the *When* of Prophetic Conditions and Mandates, we come to learn the outcome of our obedience or the consequences of our disobedience.

During the *When* of Prophetic Conditions and Mandates, God proves His faithfulness to us. Specifically, we experience the truthfulness of Ezekiel 12:25 in which God declares, "For I am the Lord: I will speak, and the word that I shall speak shall come to pass…will I say the word, and will perform it." Adam and Eve came to understand this principle as God told them that if they ate of the tree, then they would die (Genesis 3:3). We come to believe that "God is not a man that he should lie" (Num. 23:19) by seeing God allow the consequences of our actions — pleasant or unpleasant — to manifest.

Personalized Conditions and Mandates

It should be noted that some spiritual "if-then" statements that God makes to us are *personalized instructions* to the individual Believer for our particular situation. Therefore, what may be a true statement and a specific mandate for me may not work for your life. For instance, God may speak the following spiritual "if-then" statement to me: "If you quit your job, then I will bless you with a multi-million-dollar full-time ministry." Because God has presented that prophetic word to *me*, the condition of the blessing is for *me* to quit my job. If I obey, then I receive the promised blessing. In the same scenario, let us suppose someone hears my testimony concerning this matter and decides that they, too, will quit their job in the hopes that God will bless them in the same way. In their situation, because God did not necessarily speak the same mandate to them that He did to me, it is highly possible that they will not experience the same results.

God said that it is time that we as Prophetic People learn to receive our own mandates from Him. He said that, for too long, we have tried to live off the words that He has spoken to others. But, in this dispensation, it is time for His People to hear what He would say to them specifically. Because "every man must work out [our] own soul salvation with fear and trembling" (Philippians 2:12), everyone is responsible for the outcome of his or her decisions. Therefore, He said, everyone must receive his or her own personal mandate from Him.

Biblical Conditions and Mandates

In addition to the personal conditions and mandates God gives each of us, He has also given all of us universal mandates and conditions. These "global" spiritual "if-then" statements come in the form of Biblical principles. A few of these Biblical conditions and mandates are discussed below:

1. ***Principle #1: Mandates and Conditions for Salvation***
   (That) if thou shalt confess with thy mouth the Lord Jesus, and shalt believe in thine heart that God hat raised

him from the dead, [then] thou shalt be saved. – Romans 10:9

Although most Christians ascribe to the belief that "salvation is free," the Bible clearly states that there are specific mandates and conditions to receiving salvation. Therefore, when we understand the process of salvation, we realize that salvation is not an issue that is to be taken lightly. God has set in order certain steps that we must take to receive His salvation. These steps are outlined in Romans 10:9.

The first condition for salvation that God sets forth in this verse says, *"if thou shalt confess."* God requires, firstly, that we confess. To confess used in this scripture comes from the Greek word *exomologeo*, which means "to acknowledge, to agree fully, to confess, to profess or to promise". God is saying that the first condition of our salvation is for us to confess. But, one might ask, "to what are we to confess?"

The scripture says that we are to confess *"the Lord Jesus."* Note that the scripture does not say that we should confess "Jesus Christ" or even that we should confess "Jesus". Instead, God through Paul specifically mandates that we should confess *"the Lord Jesus"*. Because God always does everything "decently and in order" (I Corinthians 4:40), we can concur that God had a specific purpose in allowing Paul to phrase this verse in this manner. Specifically, there was something about confessing *"the Lord Jesus"* that is necessary for meeting the conditions required for salvation.

The word "lord" used here comes from the Greek word *kurios*, meaning "supreme in authority, sir, master, Mr.". Using this definition, when we say "Lord Jesus," not only are we acknowledging that He is Jesus, but we are recognizing Him as our authority or master. Therefore, when we *"confess the Lord Jesus,"* we are professing His Supreme Authority over our lives. We have come to the realization that we are incapable of saving ourselves and have therefore turned to Him, our only hope of "having life and that more abundantly." At this point, we therefore are relinquishing total control of our lives into His Divine Leadership. We understand that, from that point on, we do nothing unless He says to do it. We go only where He leads; we speak only what He dictates. We live as His Word commands. With our confession, we have, in fact, welcomed Jesus into our lives to reign as Lord.

The second condition of salvation detailed in this verse is that we must *"believe in [thine] heart that God hath raised him from the dead."* I have heard this verse quoted all of my life and I thought that I fully understood what it meant. However, as I began to write this section, God gave me a different revelation concerning the meaning of this portion of the scripture. Traditionally, I have taught that what this passage of scripture suggests is that we must believe that Jesus Christ was crucified, but rose from the dead. Indeed, the principles of Christianity reside upon this foundation. And, to be truthful, had their never been a crucifixion and resurrection, salvation would have been impossible. So, certainly the belief that Jesus rose from the grave is tantamount to salvation.

But, God said, we must understand the concept of His Jesus' resurrection — that is, His being *raised from the grave.* The word *raised* used here comes from the Greek word *egiro.* It means, "to waken, to rouse from sitting or lying from disease or death, from obscurity, inactivity, ruins, nonexistence". God said that that in order to be truly saved, we must come to believe in the ***resurrecting power*** of God as demonstrated through His Son, Jesus. He said that we have to know in our hearts that, no matter what situation that we are in, if we believe in Him, He is able to "raise us up". We must understand that, because we "confess the Lord Jesus", His "raising" power can pick us up when we have fallen. Because we have "professed" Him to be "the Supreme Authority of our lives", He can deliver us out of "ruin"; He can heal us from "disease". His "Divine Leadership" can take us out of "obscurity" and make a Somebody out of a Nobody. God said that when we come to believe in His resurrection powers, we are able to experience salvation on a more personal level.

After having met the compound conditions (the *"if"* portions) of this Biblical "if-then" statement, the "then" portion states that *"[we shall] be saved."* That is, once we come to *"confess with [our] mouth[s] the Lord Jesus"* and *"believe in [our] heart[s] that God raised him from the dead"*, we have met the conditions set forth by the verse. With these conditions of the biblical "if-then" statement met, God then honors His Word and, consequently, we receive salvation.

2. *Principle #2: Mandates and Conditions Concerning Deliverance*
   If my people, which are called by my name, shall humble themselves, and pray, and seek my face, and turn from their wicked ways; then will I hear from heaven, and will forgive their sin, and heal their land. – II Chronicles 7:14

II Chronicles 7:14 clearly sets forth a four-to-five-part mandate for God's people to receive deliverance. Additionally, there is a three-part consequence/conclusion. In reading this verse as a biblical "if-then" statement we can see that God is requiring us to meet the following conditions for deliverance: *humble ourselves, pray, seek His face and turn from our wicked ways.* In turn, God promised to do the following: *hear from Heaven, forgive our sin and heal our land.* God said, however, that before we can meet any of the conditions for deliverance, there is another condition implied by this verse. Specifically, He said, we must understand what it means to be His *"people, which are called by [His] Name."*

His People and His Name

What does it mean to be the People of the Lord? And, consequently, what does it mean to be called by His Name? Most people understand that the Jews are considered to be God's Chosen People. But, the Bible says that when Jesus came, others outside of the Jews were *"given the spirit of adoption"* (Romans 8:15). What this means is that while we might not be God's Chosen People by physical birth or lineage, if we receive salvation, we are in fact, God's chosen people by *spiritual rebirth.* We must understand, then, that to be called His People means that we accept and embrace our position as Jesus' Blood-bought lineage. We therefore further embrace the mandates and conditions for salvation we discussed previously, knowing that as His People, we must allow Him to rule in our lives.

So, if we are His People — we must therefore be *"called by His Name."* Although we will study names more indepth-ly in *Chapter Nine: In Pursuit of the When,* it is important for us to discuss briefly the importance of the Name of God. The word *name* comes from the Greek word *onoma,* which means "character, authority". Throughout history, the naming of a person, place or things was not to be taken lightly. This is because the meaning of the name given would "brand" the entity being named throughout its lifespan. Therefore, when the Bible says that we are called by His Name, it means that we are representing His Onoma — His Character and Supreme Authority — in our lives. In turn, each Believer is a mini facsimile of God in the earth realm. We come to think like Him; we act like Him. Our will is His Will because His Will is our will. We also move in the same demonstrations of power that He moves in (John 14;12). We do all this, not because we are so great in ourselves, but because we have come to understand as Paul did in Galatians 2:20b that it is *"yet not [us], but Christ that liveth in [us]."*

So, in review, before we can fulfill any of the conditions and mandates for deliverance in II Chronicles 7:14, we must be His People and be called by His Name. And, in order to be His People, we must and appreciate how we came to be members of His family. Moreover, to be called by His Name, we must exude His Character and Authority in our everyday lives. After meeting these "prerequisites" we are now eligible to meet the rest of the conditions for deliverance listed in the scripture.

A Humbling Experience

God said the first condition of deliverance is humility. This means that in order to receive from Him we must humble ourselves. In II Chronicles 7:14, *humble* means "to humiliate, to bring down into subjection". To illustrate the importance of humility to me, God reminded me of an incident in my childhood.

When I was growing up, we were taught to address adults as "Sir" and "Ma'am" or "Mr.", "Mrs." or "Miss". I remember that one of the worst spankings I ever received from my mother was because I addressed an adult by her first name, even though the lady told me that I could. I remember that this rule did not stop with my mother, but was probably taught to her by my grandmother who would scold us for not responding in the proper format when she asked us a question. A definitive "yes" or "no" was never good enough. Instead, we were taught to answer her "Yes, Ma'am" or "No, Ma'am." However, if we slipped up and forgot the "Ma'am", she would sometimes pretend as if she didn't hear us and re-ask the question. At other times, she would immediately scold us, saying "You'd better put a handle on that yes (or no)!"

I thought all this strange at the time, but I have now come to understand that what my mother and my grandmother were doing was instilling in me a sense of respect for and humility toward my elders and those in authority. I understand that both the title with which I addressed them and the manner in which I responded to them were outward manifestations of the attitude of humility. Those outward manifestations demonstrated to the adults that I recognized my position of subjection to them. Consequently, these manifestations also reinforced within me the realization that I was talking to an adult — my superior. As such, it would behoove me to watch what I said to him or her and the manner in which I said it. This, in turn, tended to make me mindful of how I acted in their presence.

God said that in addition to showing humility, if we truly want Him to *"hear from Heaven,"* then we must address Him properly. If we want Him to *"forgive our sins,"* we must display the attitude that it is He and He alone who is capable of doing so. If we want God to *"heal our land,* we must first acknowledge our "sickness".

Praying for Deliverance

The next condition listed in II Chronicles 7:14 is that we must *"pray."* In this verse, the word *pray* means "to intercede or make supplication." Remembering what we learned about the importance of prayer in *Chapter Two: The When of Temporary Lack*, we will simply say here that prayer is essential to receiving deliverance. It is through prayer that our humility is expressed. Also, through prayer we show God that we are spiritually mature enough to recognize and relay to Him our dire need for deliverance.

Seeking the Face of God

Immediately following the mandate to pray in II Chronicles 7:14 is the mandate to *"seek God's face."* In hearing this scripture preached as a child, I was always taught that every time we prayed, we were seeking God's face. However, in later years, God revealed to me that this was not necessarily true. As we said earlier, to pray is to intercede or to make supplication before God. Therefore, we are, in fact, telling God something or requesting Him to do something for us. While we have seen that this is certainly necessary for deliverance, God said that He is requiring a more mature level of prayer from His People, particularly from those of us who are called to a prophetic ministry.

God said that not only must we tell Him from what we wish to be delivered, but also, we must now ask His Mind on the matter; *we must now "seek His Face".* In doing so, we create an open dialogue with God whereby we are telling Him what we need for Him to hear. In turn, He tells us what He desires us to do. For too long, God said, we have relied upon Him to do all the work in our deliverance. But God said, that if we are really His People that walk in His Onoma, then we have the ability to tap into His Power within us to be delivered. But, He said, because "his ways are not our ways", we must seek His Face to receive Divine Instructions on using that power.

God said that for too long His church has had in a "gimme, gimme" mentality. We have oftentimes asked God to deliver us from something, but we never sought His Face to hear His directions concerning the deliverance.

As a result, we often are on the verge of receiving deliverance, but, because we do not pray in such a manner that we requested His input, we cannot receive the instructions for our own deliverance. God is now requiring us – His People – to seek His Face more vehemently than we ever have before…for our personal deliverance, for the healing of the land and for the salvation of a dying world.

Repenting

The final condition set forth in II Chronicles 7:14 is that we must *"turn from our wicked ways." That is, we must repent.* God said that there can be no true deliverance without repentance. When we repent, we are rendering our most sincere apology to God for the sin or transgression we have committed. We are also turning out backs on that sin, vowing never to return to it. God honors true repentance. Our sins are then "blotted out", never to be remembered again (Acts 3:19). We are then eligible to receive the deliverance and healing for which we have petitioned God.

Hearing, Healing and Deliverance

After having met the conditions in II Chronicles 7:14, we are now ready to receive the benefits of our actions. We are now in a place that God will *"hear [us] from heaven, forgive [our] sin and heal our land."*

Taking the first of the three-part conclusion, we see that God will *"hear from heaven."* But, why is it important that He hears us from heaven? The word *heaven* denotes the high spiritual place from which God reigns. Ephesians 6:12 says that in spiritual warfare, "For we wrestle not against flesh and blood, but against principalities…, against spiritual wickedness *in high places."* That means that whatever enemy we have, it is not operating on a level that we as humans can fight it alone. Instead, the warfare is taking place in a *"high place" — in the heavenlies.* Because *God is in heaven and the warfare takes place in heaven,* when we pray and God *"hear[s] [us] from heaven"*, we are sending a word directly to Him. In turn, He is able to receive our prayer at the same level as that of the warfare.

Secondly, God will now *"forgive our sin."* Because we have humbled ourselves, prayed, sought His face and repented, He has heard us from Heaven and will now forgive us for that which we have repented.

Finally, God will *"heal our land."* In the context of the scripture, the word *land* here encompasses both the physical ground upon which the Children of Israel resided and all the possessions housed on that ground. It also encompasses all the people — the Children of Israel — who resided upon the land. God said that He hears us from Heaven and does warfare on our behalf. In doing that warfare, He fights the enemy in the high spiritual places where the enemy concocts devices to keep us in bondage. God does this because the enemy tries to keep us in bondage to the same sin from which we are asking God to deliver us. Once the warfare has taken place and God has defeated the enemy, the enemy no longer has control over us in that area. Consequently, we receive deliverance in that area. However, God said, during the course of the warfare, God not only sets us free in the area about which we were praying, but the deliverance initiates a healing in other areas in our lives. Because that portion of our mind has been renewed (Ephesians 4:23), we now begin to look at other areas of our lives in a different manner. We come to understand that if God could deliver us in that area, He is able to deliver us in other areas. At that point, not only has God forgiven our sins, but He has also released a healing throughout our "land."

3. *Principle #3: Mandates and Conditions for Spiritual Living*
   "If we live in the Spirit, [then] let us also walk in the Spirit." – Galatians 5:25

The final biblical "if-then" statement we will discuss is found in Galatians 5:25. In this verse, Paul makes what seems to be a" cut-and-dried" statement. Simply put, he says that if we profess to live in the spirit, then we must walk in the spirit. When the Holy Spirit unctioned me to include this principle in this chapter, I did not quite know how I would explain this verse any clearer than it is stated in the Bible. That is because I thought I understood what it means to walk in the Spirit. To me, it seemed as if *walking in the Spirit* would be inherent in *living in the Spirit*; it seemed to be common sense. God then explained to me that there is more to this verse than meets the eye.

God said that we take for granted the concepts of both living in the Spirit and walking in the Spirit. He said that in order to truly live and walk in His Spirit, there are levels of holiness and sanctification to which we must aspire, and we must then attain. He said that we as Prophetic People have become slipshod concerning His commandments, obeying only what we want when we want. Because we represent Him in the earth, we must conduct ourselves in a manner that is both pleasing to Him and edifying the very cause and principles upon which Christianity is based. He said that we long for the deep revelations of His Word, but neglect to adhere to the simple truths. He is now calling for His people to obey Him; to be holy and sanctified in all areas of their lives and at all times. "Faith without works is dead", He said. And works done in the flesh will count for naught. We must now be about the business of being Christ-like in every fiber of our being. When we exude the Onoma of Christ in our thoughts, words and actions, we will be living in the Spirit.

Living in the Spirit versus Walking in the Spirit
God then showed me that there is a distinct difference between living in the Spirit and walking in the Spirit. In illustrating the difference between the two, God revealed a simple truth to me. He said, "*A person can live without walking, but, a person cannot walk without living.*" Admittedly, this point had never dawned on me before. And, as this revelation relates to Galatians 5:25, we see that we must first live in the Spirit *before* we walk in the Spirit.

Living in the Spirit
God then added another part to the revelation He had just given me by saying, "*A person cannot walk without living, but a person also cannot live without breathing.*" What, then, does it mean to "live in the Spirit?" The word *spirit* comes from the Greek word *pneuma*, which means "a current of air, a breath, or a blast". The word *live* comes from the Greek word *zau*, which means "to live, life, lifetime, alive, quick". Throughout the Bible, we can see that when God wants to impart His Spirit, He uses air and/wind. For instance, in Genesis 2:7, the Bible says that "God breathed into man the breath of life and man became a living soul." On the day of Pentecost in the upper room, Acts 2:2 says "there was a sound like a might rushing wind." In each of these instances, the wind or air represents the Spirit of God that, when imparted, gave life. Therefore, living in the spirit means that our sole source of life comes from God's Spirit, which resides within us. After we receive the Holy Ghost, we then live in the Spirit. God

said that anything that is alive must breathe. But, we are not necessarily *walking* in the spirit at this time.

Walking in the Spirit

God further told me, *"A person cannot walk without standing; however, a person cannot run without walking."* The word *walking* in this verse comes from the Greek word *stoicheo*, which means, "to march, in (military) rank (keep step), to conform to virtue and piety — to walk (orderly)." None of us were born knowing how to walk from birth. Instead, when babies are first born, although they may be able to move their heads and limbs, they are not capable of moving their bodies from one place to the next. Therefore, they have to be picked up and carried from place to place by someone else. During the next phase of development, they begin to roll over and, then, to crawl. After crawling, they learn to pull themselves up by holding on to stationery object (like a chair, a coffee table, or a crib). In pulling up, babies are strengthening their leg muscles, learning coordination and gaining physical stamina. After pulling up and strengthening their muscles, they are then able to stand by themselves, but, because they are still learning to balance themselves, they tend to fall down quite a bit. Finally, as babies reach a certain stage of maturity, they are then able to walk, although they are a bit unstable at first. They discover that the process of walking is simply putting one foot in front of the other, while maintaining their balance. Once they become comfortable with walking, they have become mobile and can move more quickly than when they were rolling or crawling. In walking, they also move with more assuredness than they did when they were first learning to stand. After becoming confident in their ability to walk, babies then learn how to run.

I will discuss the concepts of spiritual breathing and walking in the spirit in more detail in Book Two of the Roaring Series, *"Roaring All the Day Long: I Kept Silence (The Silence of the Limbs)."* However, because these concepts also relate to our study of the *When* of Prophetic Conditions and Mandates (particularly the if-then statement in Galatians 5:25), God directed me to share the following revelations regarding walking in the spirit:

(a) Walking in the Spirit Requires a Certain Level of Maturity.

First, He said, it is time for us as His People to get to a place of maturity in which we learn how to walk. He said that for too long, we have been as babes "desiring the sincere milk of the word." For a time and a season, God allowed us to stay in this place because He wanted to teach us at that level. But, now, He said, because of the dispensation of the anointing that we are in, we must grow up. He said that because of the urgency of the hour, we can no longer "crawl" or "roll" to get to where He wants to take us. To do so will take too long and we will miss His timing. He said that He will also not allow us to be "carried" anymore — carried by the men and women of God that He has placed in our lives to oversee us and to minister to us. The true leaders are being worn out as a result of packing around a bunch of overgrown babies. God said that it is not even enough for us to merely "stand." We must now begin to walk. He said that just as babies learn to walk by putting one foot in front of the other and maintaining their balance, we, as Believers must have our feet (our foundational teachings) shod with the preparation of the gospel of peace. Once we learn to "maneuver" the gospel — to use that which He has taught us to allow us to move to the next spiritual level — we can then put one "foot" in front of the other. We must also achieve the proper balance. In balancing ourselves, we must "rightly divide the word of truth." When we are able to coordinate these spiritual processes, we are then able to walk in the Spirit, which, simply put, means, moving from one spiritual level to the next.

(b) We Must Stand Before We Can Walk.

Regarding walking in the spirit, God also said that too many Believers want try to walk, but do not yet know how to stand. Ephesians 6:14 says "Stand, therefore, having your loins girt abut with truth..." In this verse, the word *stand* is the Greek word *histemi*, which has many meanings, one of which is "establish". To be able to stand in God means that we have a thorough understanding of who God is in us and who we are in Him. We are knowledgeable of His Word — both that in the Bible and that which He speaks to us directly. We are, in fact, "steadfast, unmovable, always abounding in the work of the Lord" (I Cor. 15:58). God said that we as a People sometimes want to walk (i.e., to move to the next level in Him), but we He will not allow us to because we our foundation (feet) is not fully established. He said that in times past, we have felt the call to a certain area of ministry and have even received prophecies that we will be successful in those areas.

However, He said, He will no longer allow His People to be placed into positions of ministry or receive blessings or elevations for which they are not spiritually ready. He said that we cannot walk before our time because we are not strong enough to support ourselves and our feet are yet "wobbly." As a result, we will fall down many times before learning how to walk. It is at this time when we are most susceptible to "being tossed about with every wind and doctrine", mistakenly thinking that we are being led by the winds of the Holy Spirit — His *Pneuma*. During this time of learning and establishing, we must be patient and know that "all things are working together for our good." We must also be willing to continue standing while we are learning to walk, knowing that, in due season, the wobbliness will cease, and we will be comfortable moving from realm to realm in the Spirit.

(c) We Must Be Mindful of Who Teaches Us to Walk.
    God said that the process and techniques by which we learn to walk in the spirit is critical to our spiritual well-being. As with babies learning to walk, we must rely on someone in authority to mentor us in our spiritual walk. Therefore, we sometimes tend to walk like the person or persons who taught us to walk. This is true for two reasons.
    First of all, our walk may be hereditary — the pace and gate with which we walk may be passed down through our bloodline. For instance, my son walks like my husband. My husband, it is said, walks like his mother's father, who did not necessarily teach my husband how to walk. There is just something in their bloodline that makes them all walk the same. Perhaps because they all come from the same lineage, maybe their physical make-ups are similar, which results in the identical movement of the legs and feet during walking. Nevertheless, they all share the same walk.
    A second reason we walk like the person(s) who taught us to walk is that we are imitating them. God said that we need to be sure of the place of worship to which we are called. We need to understand that He has assigned us specific pastors and leaders who are called to mentor us and teach us how to walk spiritually. We need to understand that person's walk and ask the Holy Spirit to reveal to us if we are to "imitate" that person's walk. God said that sometimes we submit ourselves to leadership that

is well intentioned, but whose vision is not akin to that which God has for us. Neither the leadership nor us are "bad", but the pastor-follower relationships that we have undertaken of our own accord are not necessarily ordained or sanctioned by God. As a result, we become frustrated in trying to "mimic the steps" of the leader. The frustration occurs because we are, in fact, trying to walk some place we were never intended to go!

God said we also need to be mindful of who is teaching us to walk because learning to walk requires proper supervision. Although they cannot take the steps for us, at least in our early stages of walking, our pastors and mentors must yet be there to guide us and make sure that we do not "get into anything". That is, they must be in tune with what God is doing in our lives, so that they do not allow us to venture into areas that are either ungodly or inappropriate for our ultimate purpose.

An example of this very truth can be seen in my own ministry. I know that I *am not* called to be a pastor. God has called me to be a prophetess who teaches and preaches; I understand this and am extremely comfortable with my calling. In fact, I cannot even imagine myself as a pastor! However, very early in my ministry, I sat under leaders who, because of their religious teachings and backgrounds, groomed *everyone* under their authority to become pastors. In fact, you were not considered a "real preacher" if you were not a pastor. I always knew that I was "different" but had not been taught about the prophetic nor what it meant to be called as a prophet(ess).

Can you image my discomfort in trying to "imitate" their walk, when, in fact, I was never supposed to be a pastor at all? I began to think that maybe I was crazy or something or that I was not hearing God properly. I mean, after all, these were men of God whom I had been taught to trust and reverence as a child. They were my only role models in terms of ministry. And, yet, because I was not called to a pastoral ministry, I could not follow their walk as closely as I desired. I prayed to God to send me someone with whom I could relate. God answered my prayer and released me from that ministry to sit under leadership whose walk was akin to mine. I began to learn about the prophetic call that God had upon my life. Consequently, with the right leadership, I then began to learn how to walk in my calling and, therefore, walk in the spirit.

In speaking of pastors and leaders, Hebrews 13:17 says, *"Obey them that have the rule over you, and submit yourselves: for they watch for your souls, as they that must give account, that they may do it with joy, and not with grief: for that is unprofitable for you."* Because "they watch for [y]our souls", it is imperative that we are being taught by proper leadership. Proper leadership will direct us where to walk and where not to walk. It will guide us so that we avoid pitfalls and snares. Proper leadership will also help us to cultivate a spiritual sense of direction so that we do not get lost in our walk and will always be found doing what God has called us to do. When we have sat under proper pastorals and mentors and have adhered to their teachings, we will be able to testify personally to Psalm 1:1-3, which says the following:

"Blessed is the man that **walketh** *not in the counsel of the ungodly, not* **standeth** *in the way of sinners, nor sitteth in the seat of the scornful.*

But his delight is in the law of the Lord; and in his law doth he meditate day and night.

*And he shall be like a tree planted by the rivers of water,
that bringeth forth his fruit in his season; his leaf also
shall not wither; and whatsoever he doeth shall prosper."*

(d) We Must Walk Before We Can Run.

Although Galatians 5:25 does not discuss the concept of
spiritual running, it can be concluded that spiritual
running is a natural and expected progression resulting
from proper spiritual walking. God said that just as we
must stand before we can walk, we must also walk before
we can run. He said that many of His People try to run
(i.e., to move from one realm of the spirit to the next in
great speed) but have not yet learned to walk. This is
particularly true of Prophetic People who have insight as
to what God is doing and as to what He is about to do.
Sometimes we tend to "jump the gun" and try to move
faster than we are capable of going at that time. Instead of
allowing God to teach us, correct us and prepare us at His
appointed pace, we try to speed up the process in anxious
anticipation of receiving what He has shown us we will
receive. But, because we have not grasped the concept of
walking, we sometimes lose our "balance" and/or our
"focus" when we try prematurely to run. As a result, we
sometimes "fall from grace" or "run into things" that we
are not equipped to handle. It is not that God does not
want us to run; it is simply that He wants us to know how
to walk properly before we run. Learning to run in the
Spirit requires spiritual astuteness, proper training and
much patience, as can be gleaned from the following
passage of scripture:

*"But they that wait upon the Lord shall renew their
strength; they shall mount up with wings as eagles; they
shall run, and not be weary* **[because they waited and**

previously learned to walk properly]; *and they shall walk, and not faint* **[because they waited and previously learned to stand].**" *– Isaiah 40:31*

Signs of Life within the Church

In revisiting our "if-then" statement of Romans 5:25 — *"If we live in the spirit, [then] let us also walk in the Spirit"* — we can now understand the seriousness of this prophetic mandate. God is saying to us that if we profess to live in Him — *to draw our very breath from His existence* — we should show some signs of being alive. Specifically, He said, we should walk in the spirit, thus moving from realm to realm in the spirit, showing signs of progress in our spiritual life. He said that we are to do this not only for ourselves, but to serve as the embodiment of Christ on earth. For too long, He said, the only way that the World knew that the Church was alive was because it saw them "breathing." Now, He said, the World is anxiously awaiting the manifestation of the Sons of God (Romans 8:19). To the unsaved, the Church has appeared comatose, merely laying stationery and breathing shallowly. Now, God said, the World needs to see the Church make some progress; it needs to detect some movement. The people in the World need to see the Body of Christ *stand* up and *walk* into its rightful place of authority.

THE BLESSING OF THE WHEN OF PROPHETIC CONDITIONS AND MANDATES

As we have seen, during our *Whens* of Prophetic Conditions and Mandates, God tells us what He expects of us and the results of our obedience (or the consequences of our disobedience). He then allows us to choose freely whether we will do what He says. During this *when*, we learn that although He loves us, there are requirements of us as His People. As with any strict parent, He "lays down the law" and it is up to us to conform to it. Although we may not understand His Will and His Mind at the onset, during the *When* of Prophetic Mandates and Conditions, we learn that, if we endure to the end, we will receive the promise.

8

The When of Spiritual Resurrections and Continuations

*@*ur eighth when is based on the definition of *when* which means "and then". Used in a sentence, one could say, "I had gone to bed for the night when I was awakened by a loud knock on the door." The use of the word *when* in this manner implies that, initially, there had been a sense of finality — an ending (in our example sentence, we had ended our day and had prepared to go to sleep for the rest of the night). However, there is an apparent disruption to the ending *("when I was awakened by a loud knock on the door")*. This disruption (i.e., the loud knock on the door) caused us to change our plans and to resume our previous state or activity (being awake). At this point, we have found ourselves continuing something that we had previously thought was finalized or over. Spiritually speaking, we call this *when* the *When* of Spiritual Resurrection and Continuations.

With the number eight being symbolic of new beginnings, it is fitting that we study this *when* as the eighth one on our list. During the *When* of Spiritual Resurrections and Continuations, God teaches us "it's not over until He says it's over". In this season, He also teaches us that even when we have witnessed the death or end of something with our own eyes, God, should He choose, can still resurrect or continue any situation or circumstance.

In Chapter Seven: The *When* of Prophetic Conditions and Mandates, we briefly studied the concept of resurrection. In that chapter, we discussed the word *raised* as it pertained to Romans 10:9, in which it states that the Lord Jesus was raised from the dead. We discovered that the word raised came from the Greek word *egiro*. However, in studying the word *resurrection*, we find a similar definition. Resurrection comes from the Greek word *anastasis*, which means" a standing up again; a (moral) recovery (of spiritual truth); raised to life again". *Continuation* comes from the word *continue*. *Continue* means "to maintain without interruption a condition, course or action; to stay".

During the *When* of Spiritual Resurrections and Continuations, we learn what happens "after the fact." After the fact that the doctor has told us that we only have three months to live, Jesus heals us completely. After the fact that people have verbally assaulted our character and left us "for dead", God raises us up, elevating us higher than ever before. After it has been pronounced as being all over for us in an area of our life, God shows us that He is yet God and that He must have the final say. As we become more aware of what He is teaching us during this season, we also understand that there are prophetic principles by which God operates during the *When* of Spiritual Resurrections and Continuations. Understanding these principles helps us to appreciate both what He is doing and His reasoning for doing it.

LAWS OF MOTION

In preparing to explain these principles, I prayed and asked God to show me how to relay these ideas to the reader. God then took me back to my days of studying Physics in high school and college. He told me that the premises for both spiritual resurrection and spiritual continuation are actually depicted in Sir Isaac Newton's First Law of Motion. Newton, an English physicist, studied the effects of gravity on the earth and on objects. Specifically, he studies how gravity and other outside forces affected the motion of planets and objects. From his discoveries, he composed various axioms, or laws about Physics. These laws have come to be known as Newton's Laws of Motion. These axioms, I have concluded, must have been a result of Newton receiving Divine Revelation concerning his subject matter, as they have withstood scientific scrutiny and testing, but have not been disproved to this day.

After God spoke these Laws of Motion to me, He reminded me "there is no new thing under the sun"(Ecclesiastes 1:9). He said that He has set the universe in order based on various physical laws, principles and paradigms. Those same physical laws, principles and paradigms are mirrored in the spirit realm. God said that we as a Prophetic People must seek to find the correlation between the physical laws, principles and paradigms and their spiritual counterparts. Likewise, the study of Newton's First Law of Motion as it correlates to spiritual resurrections and continuations also allows us to see that God's Laws work. Whether they concern Physics or spiritual truths; whether they come from a revered 19th century English physicist or a lowly 21st century African American prophetess, *these truths must work because they come from God.*

First Law of Motion
Newton's First Law of Motion is as follows:

Law I: "Every body continues in its state of rest, or of uniform motion in a right line, unless it is compelled to change that state by forces impressed upon it."

Newton's First Law of Motion is most commonly paraphrased/simplified in the following manner:

"An object at rest remains at rest, unless acted upon by an outside force; an object in motion remains in motion unless acted upon by an outside force."
Newton explains this law in the following manner:

> *Projectiles continue in their motions, so far as they are not retarded by the resistance of the air, or impelled downwards by the force of gravity. A top, whose parts by their cohesion and continually drawn aside from rectilinear motions, does not cease its rotation, otherwise than as it is retarded by air. The greater the bodies of the planets and comets, meeting with less resistance in freer spaces, preserve their motions both progressive and circular for a much longer time.[2]*

In this first law of motion, Newton is actually making two statements. First, he is saying that once something is still (at rest), it will not move again until something or someone (an outside force) causes it to move. Secondly, Newton is saying that once something is moving (in motion), it will not stop moving until something or someone (an outside force) causes it to stop moving. These two principles are also the same ideas upon which spiritual resurrection and spiritual continuation are based.

SPIRITUAL RESURRECTION

The first part of Newton's First Law of Motion — *"A body at rest remains at rest unless acted upon by an outside force"* — is the **Law of Spiritual Resurrection**. Spiritual resurrection occurs after something has been inactive or inoperable for so long until it is presumed dead. This something ("body") can be a ministry, a gift, a relationship, a promise from God or anything else that was once vibrant and "alive" in our lives. This is not just a gift that we don't use anymore or a ministry that we have outgrown. This is something that we do not feel that we will ever be able to use again because we feel as if it is dead; as if there is no more life in that area. That is, this "body" is no longer breathing. In Chapter Seven: The *When* of Prophetic Mandates and Conditions, we discussed "Signs of Life within the Church". We said that whenever we saw "breath, air, or wind" in the scriptures, we equate these with both life and the Spirit of the Lord. We do so, we said, because the word *spirit* comes from *pneuma*, the Greek word for breathing. Therefore, when we have an area of our life that is dead, it is totally devoid of breath — *therefore, there is an absence of God's Spirit.* In that area, there is no "breathing"; there is no "wind." There is not even a "soft breeze" to come along and give that area a gentle nudge. Consequently, without breath, there can be no life. Spiritually speaking, then, without God's Spirit, any area of our lives, that area becomes spiritually dead. Without life, *spiritual rigor mortis* sets in and that area is not only dead, but becomes "stiff." Therefore, if God's Spirit does not abide in a "body", ultimately, there can be no life and therefore, no movement (motion). The word *motion* is a derivative of the word *move*. The most commonly used form of the word move in the New Testament comes from the Greek word *kineo*. *Kineo* is the root word for *kinesis*, which is movement. *Kineo* means,"to stir, move or remove."

Spiritually and physically, when something has died, no one but God can resurrect it. Granted, God grants us the power to raise the dead (John 14:12). But, even so, resurrecting a dead entity is not something that *anyone* can do without the power and anointing of God. This is because, as we have said, life comes from the Spirit (pneuma, breath), but the Spirit comes from God. So then, even if God uses a human vessel through which to work, *there can be no resurrection* (i.e., no standing up again; no "removing" from death; no movement) *without God.* Therefore, when reading Newton's First Law of Motion from a spiritual perspective, we can see the following prophetic principle — The Law of Spiritual Resurrection:

> *A body* **(a relationship, a ministry, a promise, a gift, a prophetic assignment etc.)** *at rest* **(dead)** *will remain at rest* **(continue to be dead and lifeless)** *unless acted upon by an outside force* **(God).**

Through the Law of Spiritual Resurrection, God—*the Outside Force* – is the sole source of life and movement for the "body". Throughout the New Testament, we see that Jesus resurrected people who had died. We also see that Jesus Himself was resurrected from death. Although the choice to resurrect someone or something is at the discretion of God, we know that, even within the prophetic principle of spiritual resurrection are "sub-principles" pertaining to this subject. That is, there are deeper spiritual truths regarding spiritual (and physical) resurrection revealed in the scriptures. These truths will also give us a deeper appreciation for what God is teaching us during the *When* of Spiritual Resurrections and Continuations. Two of these sub-principles are discussed below:

1. *No matter how long something has been dead, if God chooses to resurrect it, it will live again.*

In the Bible, resurrection is not predicated upon the length of time that someone had been dead. For example, in Mark 5:41, Jesus resurrected Jairus' twelve-year-old daughter who had only been dead for a few hours. Then, in John 11:36-44, Jesus resurrected Lazarus, who had been dead for four days. I have heard atheists and unbelievers argue that the above-mentioned examples were not resurrection. In fact, they say, in both instances, neither Jairus' daughter nor Lazarus were really dead, but each was in a comatose state. This occurred, they say, because of the lack of medical technology during Biblical times; according to them, both the girl and Lazarus were misdiagnosed. Supposing that their assumptions were true, (which, we as Christians know that they are not), it would be difficult for them to apply the same argument to the resurrection in Ezekiel 37:1-14 in which God resurrects "dry bones." In this poignant example of resurrection, God gives the prophet Ezekiel a vision. In this vision God directed Ezekiel to speak to bones of corpses that had long since decomposed.

The story of Ezekiel and the Valley of the Dry Bones will be discussed in more detail in Book Three of the *Roaring Series — "My Bones Waxed Old" (Spiritual Osteoporosis).* However, the story of Ezekiel and the dry bones is also important for the purposes of our current discussion on spiritual resurrection. When Ezekiel initially prophesies to the bones (Ezekiel 37:7-8), the resurrection began to take place as follows:

> *So I prophesied as I was commanded: and as I prophesied, there was a noise, and behold a shaking, and the bones came together, bone to his bone.*
>
> *And when I beheld, lo, the sinews and the flesh came up upon them, and the skin covered them above: but **there was no breath in them.***

Ezekiel understood that just because the bones had re-joined and were recovered with skin, they were still devoid of *life*. This is because, as we discussed earlier, there was yet no *pneuma* — no breath from the Spirit of

God — within them. As Ezekiel continued to prophesy, God directed him to prophesy to the wind:

Then said he unto me, Prophesy unto the wind, prophesy, son of man, and say to the wind, Thus saith the Lord God; Come from the four winds, O breath, and breathe upon these slain, that they may live.

So I prophesied as he commanded me, and the breath came into them, and they lived, and stood up upon their feet, an exceeding great army. **Ezekiel 37:9-10**

God told Ezekiel that the vision of the dry bones was representative of the "house of Israel" (Ezekiel 37:11). God then directed Ezekiel to prophesy to the Children of Israel regarding further spiritual resurrection. Speaking through Ezekiel, God assured them that, although they felt hopeless and dead, He was sending a spiritual resurrection to them in the following manner:

Therefore prophesy and say unto them, Thus saith the Lord God; Behold, O my people, I will open your graves, and cause you to come up out of your graves, and bring you into the land of Israel.

And ye shall know that I am the Lord, when I have opened your graves, O my people, and brought you up out of your graves,

*And shall put my spirit in you, and ye shall live, and I shall place you in your own land: then shall ye know that I the Lord have spoken it, and performed it, saith the Lord. – **Ezekiel 37:12-17***

The *When* of Spiritual Resurrections and Continuations can be a time of exhilaration and surprise as we come to understand that, despite what it looks like, "things are not over." For instance, after waiting so long for God's Promises to manifest in our lives, we may have become weary and reluctant to believe for those promises any longer. As a result, we may not allow God to speak to us in those areas for fear that He will continue to give us unfulfilled hope.

Specifically, we are afraid He will tell us that the promises are going to manifest, but, as usual, to no avail. Because we have chosen to not expose that area to God (i.e., to His Spirit; pneuma; air), that area "suffocates" and dies. Consequently, when it dies, a small part of who we are in Christ also dies with it. So, at that point, we have accepted the (premature) death of those promises. Granted, we are not happy with the death of that area; we may even mourn and grieve its loss. Nevertheless, we put it behind us and try to go on as best we can. We alter our mindset so as not to desire the manifestation of those promises anymore; we busy ourselves thinking about other things. "Maybe that wasn't God after all," we say. "Maybe I missed my season; this is probably all that I will ever have." We adapt to life without that part of ourselves and determine to go on "anyhow" ...*when, all of a sudden*...God resurrects those promises. He speaks to that dead area and commands it to "Come forth!" He "unburies" it, "stands it up" and demands that it live again. Then, God "breathes into it the breath of life". That which was dead is now alive again! The desire for the manifestation of those promises is back, now stronger than ever. With the new life comes new determination within us to receive those promises and to seek God's Will for our lives as never before.

Although this *when* is a *when* of new beginnings, change is not always welcome. Sometimes we become accustomed to things being dead. It is not that we wanted areas of our lives to die, but, after they died, we learned to live without them. During the *When* of Spiritual Resurrections and Continuations, it sometimes feels as if God is "re-hashing old wounds" by resurrecting things in our lives that at one time seemed to cause us great pain and frustration. We understand that the resurrection is of God, but because we do not want to be disappointed or frustrated again, we sometimes resist the change that this resurrection will cause us to have to make. God is saying that if we would yield to Him and allow Him to complete the resurrection process, although there may be minimal pain, the victory of the outcome will far outweigh any pain or frustration that we might experience.

2. **When God kills something, no one can resurrect it and it will never live again.**

Although, God is merciful and "slow to anger" (Psalm 103:8), there is also a vengeful aspect of God. In fact, there are many Biblical examples in which God (or, God through Jesus) killed living entities. One example is found in Mark 11:12-14 in which Jesus passes by a fig tree that was not bearing fruit. He cursed the tree to die. The tree withered and, from that day forward, the fig tree did not bear any more figs (Mark 11:20-21). Another example is found in the story of Ananias and Sapphira (Acts 5:1-10). Both Ananias and his wife Sapphira kept part of some monies received for selling certain possessions. Although Ananias and Sapphira owned the possessions, the entire amount of the money from the sale was earmarked for the work of the ministry. Because each of them tried to deceive God by giving a lesser amount, each was struck dead as they went to give their offering.

During the *When* of Spiritual Resurrections and Continuations, we learn to sense when God is awakening areas of our lives that we had assumed to be inactive. However, during this time, we also learn to differentiate between God resurrecting something and the enemy trying to re-awaken something that God Himself has killed in us. Perhaps it is a bad habit or an ungodly desire. Perhaps it is a wrong way of thinking or a deep emotional wound. Whatever it is, if God has killed it, we must let it go. We must also understand that if God took it away from us, we did not need it in the first place. Therefore, during the *When* of Spiritual Resurrections and Continuations, we must be in tune with the Holy Spirit to ascertain whether the resurrection we sense is of God or from the enemy.

SPIRITUAL CONTINUATIONS

Returning to our discussion of Newton's First Law of Motion, let us now examine the second half of the law. Paraphrased, it states, *"An object in motion will remain in motion unless acted upon by an outside force."* Newton goes on to give an example of this portion of the law. First, he explains, anything that has been projected or thrown will continue to move as long as there is no air resistance or as long as they can stay in the air without gravity pulling them down. Next, he uses the analogy of a spinning top. He says that because the top has a round shape, it is made to continue to rotate unless the air "retards" it or slows it down. He then gives the example of the planets, saying that as long as there is nothing to stop them, the planets will continue to rotate and to move throughout the universe without colliding.

Throughout the course of the book, we have discussed various spiritual seasons. We understand that, all seasons

— those that are spiritual and those that are chronological (i.e., autumn, winter, spring, summer) — have an appointed beginning and ending. Likewise, there are certain relationships, ministries and other areas of our lives upon which God has placed limits and deadlines. That is, He gives us a certain amount of time in which we must allow Him to perfect those "bodies." Usually, once that time has past, if those parts of us are not perfected, He allows the season in which that work was to be done to end. However, during the *When* of Spiritual Resurrections and Continuations, God "stops the clock" and allows us more time to "get our affairs in order." During these times, He holds back the *spiritual gravity* — *"death and the grave"* — that would slow us down. He also abates the *strong winds*, so that we are not "tossed to and fro, and carried about with every wind of doctrine" (Ephesians 4:14). He eliminates all obstacles, so that we have nothing over which to stumble; His Word becomes "a lamp unto [our] feet and a light unto [our] path" (Psalm 119:105). In the absence of "gravity" and "wind retardation", we are placed on a well-lighted path en route to God's Divine Purpose for us in that area of our lives. We are then free to "remain in motion", continuing to do what we need to do to finish our assigned task for that season.

Let us now revise the second half of Newton's First Law of Motion from a spiritual standpoint. The revised (prophetic) law is called *The Law of Spiritual Continuations*. It would read in the following manner:

*A body (**a relationship, a ministry, a promise, a gift, a prophetic assignment, etc.**) in motion (**stirring, breathing**) will remain in motion (**continuing to stir and breathe**) unless it is acted upon by an outside force (**God**).*

God said that there are some "bodies" that are already dead that He has to resurrect. But, He said, there are other "bodies" that are far from dead, but need to continue in motion so that they can fulfill their predestined purpose. The latter group of "bodies" is in need of a *Spiritual Continuation.* Continuations are a miraculous time in which endings are "held at bay" until a desired end is achieved. The story of Joshua and his defeat of the Amorites at Gibeon is an example of a continuation. In Joshua 10:12-14, Joshua and the Children of Israel were at war with the Amorites. Understanding that he needed more daylight time to fight, Joshua prophesied to the sun, ordering it to "*Stand thou still* upon Gibeon." Likewise, he ordered the moon to *stand still* "in the valley of Ajalon" (Joshua 10:12). Joshua understood that, it was a law of natural physics that the sun would go down after an appointed number of hours. The moon would then be visible but would not be adequate light with which to complete the battle. He also understood the importance of prophetic precision and timing. He knew that it was "now or never." Specifically, he understood that that day was the appointed time in which he and the Children of Israel were to defeat the Amorites. It was not to be the next day or even that night. No, it had to be that day! Joshua knew that he would do all that he could do in the time in which he had to do it, but even then that would still not be enough time. Joshua realized that he needed a miracle; *he understood that he needed a continuation.*

Likewise, there are some things that we cannot afford to have end until such time as we have accomplished the purpose for which God has sent those areas. For instance, there are some relationships that, try as we might to get rid of the other person, God still allows that person to come into our lives. He does so because there is yet something that we are to impart to them and visa versa. Sometimes, there are ministries that we feel we have outgrown and are ready to leave. But, God sends a season of continuation within that ministry; there may yet be something that He wants to teach us or a ministry contact that we must make that will help us on the next level. Whatever the "body", God keeps it in motion until He says it is time for something else to happen.

Translation

In addition to spiritual *resurrection* and spiritual *continuation*, there is also spiritual *translation*. Specifically, translation involves being instantly changed from a physical being to a spiritual being. Translation is depicted in Hebrews 11:5, which says, "By faith Enoch was *translated* that he should not see death, and was not found, because God had *translated* him…" It is also the same process by which Moses was taken up to heaven and Elijah was carried away on a chariot. The process of translation literally skips death. That is, there is no retiring of the physical vessel to enter the spirit realm. In fact, both the physical vessel and the spirit are taken away during translation, so that there is no need for resurrection nor a vessel in which resurrection could occur.

God said that there are some "bodies" that He will not allow to die. Instead, He will continue them, but on another spiritual level. In order to do so, He must *translate* them.

I have a personal understanding of the principle of translation through a relationship with a former spiritual leader. In my earlier years of ministry, this person served as a pastor, a spiritual mother and a prophetic role model. However, as I began to grow in the ministry and in my walk with the Lord, I realized that the role that I would play in her ministry would have to change in order for My Divine Purpose to be fulfilled. As a result, I began to fear the "death" of our relationship. This fear actually kept me paralyzed for so long because I did not want to lose the closeness we once had. She even told me that the time would come when God would change our relationship and that I would have to "grow up" and stand on my own in Him. As time went on, I stepped out on my own, afraid to lose that relationship, but determined to do what God had called me to do. To my chagrin, the relationship could not *continue* as it was. However, to my amazement, the relationship also did not *die*. Instead, it was *translated* into a different, stronger bond. At my present level of spiritual maturity, the relationship is no longer that of pastor-protégé. Instead, it has now transformed to that of friends and covenant partners. Because God ordained that relationship, it will never die but will be translated to serve God's Purpose for the relationship on any spiritual plane.

GOD'S SPONTANEOUS ASPECT

The *When* of Spiritual Resurrections and Continuations is a *when* in which we see the spontaneous aspect of God manifested. During this *when*, we are reminded that we serve a God of such awesome omnipotence that He can resurrect our dead situations and circumstances. We also learn He can give us unlimited illumination of His Word to complete His Assigned Tasks in His Desired Timing. He does so knowing that there is a season coming in which we will not be able to complete the task; He knows that "night cometh, when no man can work" (John 9:4).

9

In Pursuit of the When

od said that it is not enough merely to know that the *whens* in the previous eight chapters exist, but we must understand how to apply these whens to our lives. I prophesy to you by the unction of the Holy Ghost that if we are to fulfill God's Purpose in our lives, we must *recognize, name, embrace,* and *remember* our *whens*.

RECOGNIZING THE WHEN

The first stage of revelation concerning our spiritual seasons is that of *recognizing the when*. At this stage, we come to the realization that something of spiritual significance is taking place in our lives. We receive revelation that a *when* — a season — has actually taken place. We conclude that "This [whatever the *when* was] happened for a reason" although we may not be sure what the reason was.

Now, while this sounds simple on the surface, the question must yet be asked, "How do we *recognize* a *when*?" The word *recognize* comes from the root word "cognizant" which means "to be aware of". God is saying that we need to be *aware* of our *whens*; *aware* of what He is doing in our lives. We must be, He said, *aware* of our seasons.

God showed me that the concept of recognizing a *when* is, to a large degree, the foundation upon which much of our spiritual growth is based. Especially as a Prophetic People, we cannot afford to go through entire seasons undaunted and without gaining the spiritual insight God intended for us to glean from the *whens*.

God said that, for too long, the Church has gone about our spiritual walk haphazardly. We have sought His Direction, He said, but only in part and only to the degree that we have cared to follow — only following when it is comfortable/convenient to do so. We have become complacent and, although we *say* we seek to know God's Will for our lives, we do not put forth the effort and level of sacrifice to know Him as we truly should. We have followed Him and obeyed His "surface" directions in the past. However, God said He is now requiring every Child of God to "press into Him" and to hear His specific instructions for us at every phase of our spiritual walk.

Those of us who will be used mightily of Him can no longer wait as the Children of Israel did for a "Moses" to bring down the edicts of God to us (Exodus 32:23). We must now become *active participants* in the quest for Divine Revelation that pertains to our own lives. We must develop a "hunger and thirst after righteousness" (Matthew 5:6) as never before. We must be as Paul and desire to know Him in all of His attributes (Philippians 3:10). And, in doing so, we will develop a more regimented level of prophetic discipline that can only be nurtured and cultivated through much prayer, consecration and intimate fellowship with God. We will then allow Him to train our spiritual eyes to see past the physical realm of a situation or circumstance. We will also allow God to train our spiritual ears to tune out all other voices, homing in upon His Voice and His mandates for our lives ("*my sheep know My Voice and a stranger's voice they will not follow*" [John 10:4-5]). We will sharpen our senses to pick up His presence and His "aura". We will yield our very thought processes to Him so that His Word supersedes our intellect, logic and knowledge (Philippians 3:8) We will develop the ability to block out everything else and concentrate on Him. He said that the culmination of the "processes" will become practice ("Pray without ceasing" [I Thessalonians 5:17]). Moreover, the "habitual" practice in turn will become a lifestyle. And, that lifestyle will eventually becomes so familiar to us that we will no longer have to struggle to know if God is speaking to us because we will be in tune with Him on a regular basis. Consequently, during situations and circumstances in which He is trying to get our attention, we will be *cognizant* of the fact that He is speaking to us. We will be *aware* that He is trying to show us something; we will then *recognize* our *whens*.

There are different levels of *when* recognition. Two levels are as follows:

Pardon Me, When, But, Don't I Know You from Somewhere?

One level of when recognition can be derived from the definition of the word *recognize* which means "to perceive to be something previously known". Here, the word *recognize* implies foreknowledge or past experience with that that is being re-encountered. In this definition of *recognize* there is a certain sense of familiarity. "But," one might ask, "how can we be familiar with the *when* upon first encountering it?" The answer lies not in our experiences, but in those of Jesus Christ.

In Isaiah 53:5, the Bible tells us the following:

"But he was wounded for our transgressions, he was bruised for our iniquities; the chastisement of our peace was upon him: and with his stripes are we healed.

Likewise, Romans 8:29 says:

*"For whom **he did foreknow,** he also did predestinate to be conformed to the image of his Son, that he might be the firstborn among many brethren"*

Also, Philippians 2:5-6 says:

"Let this mind be in you, which was also in Christ Jesus:

Who, being in the form of God, thought not robbery to be equal with God:"

Though we often take it for granted, we — the *Church*-are the Body of Christ. We are an extension of Him, connected to the same source of life - God, with the same blood running through us. Therefore, being connected to Him, we experience *everything* that He has experienced — both pleasant and unpleasant. Therefore, as Isaiah 53:1-10 depicts, because He loved us and chose to suffer for us, most Believers will never have to go through the physical torment and brutality that He experienced at Calvary. However, His physical sufferings will be manifested in our lives as spiritual sufferings.

However, as we grow spiritually and strive to be more like Him, He allows us to become cognizant of His sufferings and His experiences. He does this by allowing us to experience *whens*. We must therefore come to a level of spiritual maturity where we say, "Yes, I am going through something, but it is nothing that Christ — my Head — has not gone through before." Once we associate our current experience with that which He experienced in times past, we have come to the place where we have learned to recognize our *when*.

Not only are we the Body of Christ, but Revelations 22:17 says that we are also the *Bride* of Christ. In speaking of marriage the Bible declares that "And they twain [the man and the woman] shall become one flesh… "(Mark 10:8). So, even as the Bride of Christ, the concept of our being one with Him still holds true. Just as in physical marriages, the relationship that we have with Christ as His Bride is one of intimacy and intense communication — both spoken and non-verbal.

For instance, my husband has an uncanny knack for knowing when something of importance is on my mind. Whether that "something" is causing me happiness, worry, frustration or anxiety, my husband can sense that something is going on. Not wanting to worry him, I try my best to hide it whenever I am going through something. I get very quiet and try to "keep a stiff upper lip." But, sooner or later, he very patiently and gently asks me, "What's wrong?" Because he is one with me, although he might not be able to pinpoint the problem (which is "**naming** the *when*", which we will discuss in the next section), he is still able to ascertain that **something** is awry. And, it works the same way with me. Because I am his wife, I can sense when something is taking place inside of him.

Likewise, we too as the Bride of Christ must attain such a level of oneness with Christ until we can readily denote signs of His suffering *in our own lives*. We must learn to recognize what He is trying to say to us; we must learn to recognize our *when*.

When, I Really Appreciate You!

A second level of recognizing a *when* can be found in another definition of the word *recognize* which means "to acknowledge with a show of appreciation." This definition is most commonly associated with awards/certificates of appreciation "given in recognition of" various services or efforts. When we recognize someone for his or her efforts or accomplishments, we are actually saying, "I appreciate the results you accomplished in this area." We are acknowledging that the means notwithstanding, the result was *good*.

God is saying that we must learn to appreciate our *when* — no matter how unpleasant or painful the *when* may be. We must learn to appreciate our *whens* because they come from God. Therefore, the end result must be *good*. Paul understood this prophetic principle when he wrote the following:

> *"And we know that **all things** work together for **good** to them that love God, to them who are the called according to his purpose."* – **Romans 8:28**

A poignant Biblical example of appreciation of a *when* can be found in the story of Joseph. Joseph, after being sold into slavery by his brothers and then falsely imprisoned for years, is miraculously placed into a position of power and authority in Egyptian government. Many years later, Joseph has the opportunity to "make or break" the very brothers who were responsible for his demise as they come to him asking for food during a famine. When Joseph tells them who he is, they become afraid that he is angry with them because of their cruelty toward him. Joseph, having gained Divine Revelation concerning his situation gave the following reply:

> *"But as for you, ye thought evil against me; but God meant it unto good, to bring to pass, as it is this day, to save much people alive.*
>
> *Now therefore, fear ye not: I will nourish you, and your little ones. And he comforted them and spake kindly to them."* – **Genesis 50:20-21**

When we develop the mindset of appreciating our *when*, we come to understand that there is no such thing as a "bad" *when*. Like Paul and Joseph, we accept the fact that no matter how painful, uncomfortable or unpleasant the *when*, we must respect its place in our lives at that point. We must *recognize* it for what it is; a vehicle created by God to take us to the next level of the Divine Purpose for our lives.

NAMING THE WHEN

The second stage of revelation concerning our spiritual whens is that of *naming* the *when*. At the *"naming-the-when"* stage, not only have we now *recognized* the *when*, but we now understand *why* God allowed this season of our lives to come to pass. At the *"recognizing-the-when"* stage, we "knew that something was going on, but we couldn't put our finger on it." But, at the *"naming-the-when"* stage, we have identified the *when* and are in tune with the specific lesson God is trying to teach us in it. In fact, we are so much in tune with it that we are able to "title" it; to give it a name. It is in this stage of prophetic revelation that God's Will for this season is revealed to us. The "light bulb" comes on in our spirits and we realize, "Aha! So, *this* is what God was trying to teach me all along!"

As I prayed about how to illustrate this point, God showed me autumn, winter, spring and summer. He then asked me, "How can you tell winter from spring? Or, summer from fall?"

I answered, "I can tell them apart by the temperature and the atmospheric conditions. Also, I know that certain events taken place during certain seasons. For instance, in autumn, leaves fall off the trees and school starts. In winter, Christmas is celebrated."

God then said that we know what the seasons are because we have been taught to expect certain characteristics of each season. Because of the consistency of the seasons, year in and year out, since the beginning of time, the same occurrences have taken place during the same season in the same manner. He said that because we have previously experienced them, we are well acquainted with the nuances of each one. We are then able to name the seasons based on both our personal experiences with them and what we have been taught based on the experiences of others. Likewise, we must develop a spiritual means of naming our *whens*.

"What's In a Name?"

The word *name*, when used as a noun (e.g., a *name*), is derived from the Greek word *onoma*, which literally means "name; authority; character". The verb form of the word *name* (example: *naming* the *when*) comes from the Greek word *onomazo*. It means "to assign a name or to call". So, then, we see that the act of naming someone or something is not to be taken lightly, since the name chosen denotes the very character or authority of the person or entity being called. Likewise, the process of naming our *whens* is one that should be of a prayerful undertaking.

Throughout both the Old and New Testaments, the names assigned to the men and women of the Bible proved to foretell their purposes and destinies within the Kingdom of God. Some examples are as follows:

Abraham, whose name was changed from Abram - The name *Abraham* means "populous; father of a multitude". He would become the father of many nations, and later have the lineage of Jesus Christ to come through him.

Sarah, whose name was changed from Sarai. - The name *Sarah* means "female noble; princess, queen". As the wife of Abraham, she bore their son, Isaac when she was more than 90 years old. As her name suggests, she became the mother of many nations and, as mother of Isaac, bore children that eventually became the lineage of Jesus Christ.

Moses - Moses, for instance, whose name means "drawn out" was taken from the Nile River by the Pharaoh's daughter after having been placed in a basket by his mother. Later, Moses was the person God used to "draw" His People out of Egypt.

Jesus understood the importance of assigning the proper name. He demonstrated His knowledge of this when he repeatedly asked Peter concerning the people:

"...Whom do men say that I the Son of man am?" *– Matthew 16:13b*

And He reiterated the point when He personalized the question, asking Peter:

"He saith unto them, But whom say ye that I am?" *– Matthew 16:15*

Likewise, Peter in answering, displayed his understanding of Christ's true character — His *onoma* — His *name*: *"And Simon Peter answered and said, Thou art the Christ, the Son of the living God." – Matthew 16:16*

This passage of scripture has always amused me. I can visualize poor Peter, seemingly being repeatedly asked the same question by Jesus. No doubt, after the first two times, Peter wondered why Jesus would keep asking the same question. "Perhaps He did not hear me clearly the first time," maybe Peter thought. "Or, maybe He's looking for a specific answer." As is human nature, I can imagine that Peter was probably getting somewhat frustrated and nervous. "After all," Peter probably thought, "if omnipotent and all-knowing Jesus does not know the answer to this question, can *any* answer I give Him be correct?"

Unbeknownst to Peter, there was a prophetic purpose to Jesus' actions. Finally, after Jesus' last time asking Peter what the people thought of Him (versus who He is/was), He threw in a new twist. He asked Peter — the Rock — who he had come to know Jesus to be. It was not that all knowing, omnipotent, God-made-flesh Jesus did not already know what Peter would say before even Peter knew what was going to come out of his mouth. Nor did Jesus need Peter to boost His ego by telling Him repeatedly how wonderful the people nor Peter thought He was. Instead, Jesus was putting into place the very foundation upon which our faith today is based. Jesus wanted Peter — *the Rock* — *the Church* — to be able to verbalize who He was/is to it. As Jesus said in Matthew 12:34 said, "for out of the abundance of the heart, the mouth speaketh." To the point, He had to make sure that the Church had the right heart; that it knew who He was/is and what its purpose would be.

In fact, it could be said that Jesus' mission would have been incomplete had He not gotten the Church to the point where it could actually verbalize who He was. In other words, if Christians were going to represent Him in the earth realm after His departure; if they were going to fight the good fight of faith; if they were to be called by His name — **Christians** — they had to first *know who He was*.

And, if they were to win others to the Kingdom, they had
to be able to *tell others* His True Identity. Finally, in order
to be able to stand in times of adversity and spiritual
warfare, they had to be able to, as David decreed,
"encourage themselves in the Lord." That is, they had to
be able to tell *themselves* who He was.

Consequently, God said, it is no different for the Church
of today. I prophesy to you by the unction of the Holy
Ghost that if the Body of Christ is to come into maturity
and assume its rightful place of power and authority, we
too, like Saints of old, must have a realization of who
Christ is. God is saying that we must not only lend lip
service to Christianity but are now required to exemplify
the *onoma* — the character and authority — of Christ, now
more than ever before. It is not enough merely to have
knowledge of His name; we must now demonstrate that
knowledge, allowing that revelation to yield physical
manifestations in our lives (for faith without works is
dead). We must now "speak" His name; we must now
"live" His name. For, God said, in His Name is our very
salvation; our existence; our purpose for being:

"And she [Mary, mother of Jesus] shall bring forth a son,
and thou shalt call his name **JESUS: for he shall save**
his people from their sins.

Now all this was done, that it might be fulfilled which
was spoken of the Lord by the prophet, saying,

Behold, a virgin shall be with child, and shall bring forth
a son, and they shall call his name **Emmanuel,** *which*
*being   interpreted   is,   **God   with   us.**"*
– Matthew 1:21-23

*Wherefore God also hath highly exalted him [Jesus], and given him **a name which is above every name:***

*That **at the name of Jesus** every knee should bow, of things in heaven, and things in earth, and things under the earth;*

And that every tongue should confess that Jesus Christ is Lord, to the glory of God the Father. **– Phillippians 2: 9-11**

And whatsoever ye shall ask in my [Jesus'] name, that will I do, that the Father may be glorified in the Son.

*If ye shall ask any thing **in my name**, I will do it."* – **John 14: 13-14**

Therefore, it is necessary for the Church to be able to name who Jesus is. It also necessary for us to be able to name our *whens.*

How Do We Name a When?

Having discussed the importance of allocating the proper names to people, we can now speak with more in-depth understanding of assigning the proper names to our *whens.* When we can demonstrate our understanding of exactly where God has us in our spiritual walk, we are well on our way to learning the lesson He desires to teach us in that place. We have come to the point where we understand the character of the *when* — we are ready to assign it a name.

But how do we go about doing this? God revealed to me that in naming our *when*, we must apply certain spiritual revelations to our when to assign it the proper names. In doing so, God reveals to us various principles used in naming a *when* that are akin to the techniques used to assign physical names. Specifically, just as with names of physical entities, a *when* is assigned a name based on its *lineage, gender* and *"physical" attributes*.

a. Lineage

A *when* can be named according to its lineage. In the English language, we determine the lineage of practically all words and names. Etymology, for instance, is the study of words that gives meaning to a word based on that word's etymological origin or what other words were combined to make that word. For instance, in the word *hatbox*, the words *hat* and *box* have been combined to make this word. In naming humans, our culture assigns a surname (also called a proper name) to every person when they are born. Traditionally, this surname is taken from the father's lineage and becomes the child's *last name.* Just as we have a surname or last name that denotes our lineage, so do *whens* have places of origin. Consequently, because a *when* is a spiritual season, it must come from a spiritual lineage. Therefore, we must receive spiritual revelation as to the *when's* place of origin or its assigned purpose before we can ascribe an accurate "surname."

At this point, one might say, "I thought you said earlier that all *whens* come from God." And, indeed, this is true. So, in a general sense, all *whens* share the same place of origin. Therefore, one might ask, if all *whens* come from the same point of origin, why would they not all share the same lineage and, therefore, have the same surname? If this train of thought were true, it would also be true that, because every person on the earth came from God (through Adam and Eve), we should all have the same surname. Or, all persons with the first name of John would have the same surname. Obviously, neither of these two statements are true. Again, God appreciated the value of the proper name so much until He Himself assigned various surnames to men and women in the Bible based on His Divine Purpose — not only for their lives, but for their seed; their lineage. An example of this can be seen in God's meticulous directions to Joseph for the naming of the Tribes of Israel (Genesis 49). Even in this scenario, it can be noted that while all the tribes had come from the same father — Jacob — God gave them all a different name according to His Divine Purpose for each of their lineages. It should also be noted that in naming the tribes, God specified that the first name of each of Israel's sons be used as a name for the tribes (Judah, Levi, etc.). However, as that tribe grew, that first name later became a surname for those who would come after (house of Judah, etc.).

This is why there may be various versions of the same eight *whens* discussed in previous eight chapters. The premise (definition) is the same, but they may serve different purposes (may have different first names). For example, during a specific season God may be teaching us prophetic principles relating to our spiritual growth. Specifically, He may want to multiply our joy in our spiritual life (walking with Him, serving in ministry, etc.). To do this, He may allow us to experience the *When* of Alternative Means. To name this *when* using the last name (Surname) first, we might call it, "The *When* of Alternative Means (Surname [first]) in which God multiplied my joy in my spiritual life (First Name [last])". Suppose, then, that a few months later, we experienced problems in our marriage; maybe the joy had gone out of it. God may choose to allow us to experience the When of Alternative Means again, but this time, because He would obtain a different result, we would name the *when* differently. This time, we might name this *when* "The *When* of Alternative Means (Surname) in which God Multiplied the Joy in my Marriage (First Name)". As we can see, it is, in essence, the same *when*, but God used it to accomplish a different purpose. As such, we say that the same *when* had a different first name.

b. "Physical" Characteristics

In addition to being named according to their lineage, *whens* can also be named according to their physical characteristics and abilities. The naming of people according to physical characteristics and abilities is a practice that has taken place since Biblical times. Adam, whose name means "ruddy", was so named because his flesh had a red hue to it, having just been made from soil of the same color. Esau, whose name means "hairy" was given his name based on his hairy appearance. To be able to name a *when* in this manner, we must ask ourselves the following questions:

1. *What does it look like?* Does it look "sad"? If so, maybe God is trying to teach us how to handle some painful situation we have experienced. Does it look "short"? If it does, maybe God is revealing one of our shortcomings to us. Whatever the characteristic, we must be spiritually astute enough to see what the *when* looks like and allow God to give us a name for it.

2. *What does it do?* – Does it teach? Does it reprimand? Does it exhort? In naming a *when* based on it abilities, we are speaking why the *when* was assigned to our lives. The ability to name a *when* in this manner requires us to be able to discern spiritually, seeing exactly what God wants this when to accomplish in our lives.

c. Gender

The last naming convention we will discuss is that of gender-based naming. In the naming of people, gender-based naming is probably the most common naming convention used. In our society, there are certain names that are typically reserved for females — Mary, Jane, Lisa, etc. Likewise, there are other names that are typically reserved for men — John, James, Paul, etc. Although there are no legal restrictions as to what first name a parent can give a child, it is considered socially inappropriate to, say, name a daughter John or a son Mary. We have come to associate names with genders because of their usage by a particular gender throughout the years. In turn, these names were used by a particular gender as a result of their Biblical and/or historical meanings. That is, at some point in the origin of these names, their meanings were ascribed based on the principles of the roles, responsibilities and attributes of males and females within our society. For instance, my son Desmond's name means, "ruler of the mound." The name *Desmond* is considered to be a male name. This is because the act of ruling was considered to be a male responsibility.

Granted, there are female derivatives of male names, (Paula, for instance, is derived from Paul). Nevertheless, in these instances, the addition of a suffix (the "a" at the end of Paul) denotes femininity. When this occurred in times past, the female being named was usually being named in honor of her father or some male in her family. The naming of a female in such a manner was done to pay homage to that male. However, because the suffix was added to the name, the name was yet considered female and was therefore socially accepted.

A *when* can also be assigned a gender-based name. But to do this, we must first ascertain whether a *when* is male or female. We must learn to name our *whens* based on gender; we must understand if they are male or female. The Hebrew word for male is *zakar*. It means, "remembered" and denotes the most noteworthy males. The Greek word for male is *asen*, which means, "stronger, for lifting". The latter definition speaks to the physical ability of a male, particularly the male physical strength being superior to that of a female. The Hebrew word for female is *neqebah*. The Greek word for female is *thelus*, which is derived from the root word *thelazo*, which means "nursing an infant". Biblically, males and females were assigned different roles. The role of the male was seen as that of being the provider, establishing order, ruling and administering correction. The role of the female was seen as that of birthing and nurturing.

God said in ascertaining the gender of a *when*, we need to know what its role is in our lives. That is, is this a season in which God wants to nurture us in an area, or to birth something into our spirit? If so, then the *when* is *female*. Or, is this a season in which God wants to show us that He can provide for us, or wishes to correct us? If this is the case, then we are experiencing a *male when*. Once we can correctly ascertain the gender of this when, we are able to assign it an appropriate gender-based name.

Naming a *when* can be an arduous task. There are many questions we must ask, both of ourselves and of God. There are also many factors about the season to be considered. Nevertheless, it is crucial to our spiritual growth that we properly name the *when*. In doing so, every time we speak its name, we are acknowledging that we understand exactly what season we are in and what God is doing at that point in our lives.

EMBRACING THE WHEN

Having recognized and named the *when*, we are now tasked with the responsibility of applying the lesson learned to our lives. That is, we must now *embrace* the *when*. In the "embracing-the-*when*" stage, we are, in effect saying, "I thank God for what I just went through; I learned from it and will now be able to help others who are going through the same thing."

Defined, *embrace* means, "to clasp in the arms: to hug; to cherish, love; to encircle, enclose; to accept". God told me that it is not merely enough to be cognizant of the presence or occurrence of a spiritual season. Nor, He says, is it enough to give it a name. At the "embracing-the-*when*" stage, we are now tasked with the responsibility of applying the lesson learned to our lives. God showed me that there are at least three steps in embracing.

When we embrace something physical, the first step we take is open our arms. In doing so, we are actually doing several things. First, we are reaching out for the person or entity that is being embraced. In opening our arms, we are also letting down our defenses and becoming vulnerable to whom or what we are about to embrace. And, if our arms are open, we have exposed our upper torso (our chest, heart, etc.) and cannot readily defend ourselves from the person or entity we are about to embrace. We are exposing the person or entity to what is called our "personal space." This means that there is a high degree of trust for that person or entity. Thirdly, when we open our arms, we are welcoming the person or entity we are about to embrace. We are, in effect, making space for it and welcoming it to come to us.

Likewise, in embracing a spiritual *when*, we must also open ourselves up to receive it and, therefore, to receive what God is doing at that time in our lives. Sometimes it seems like God chooses the most awkward of times to perform various tasks in our lives. Nevertheless, we must allow Him to do what He wants when He wants. After we recognized the *when*, we understood that this season was of God. After we named the *when*, we knew exactly what He was doing. But, now that we are embracing the *when*, we must welcome this season. We must reach out for it and let our defenses down. Then, we must let it enter our "personal space" — the deep places of our spirit in which we have put up defenses. These are the places in which we do not allow anyone. These may be places of great pain. Or, they may be places of insecurity and intimidation. They may even be places of utter humiliation and desolation. However, no matter how much discomfort we may experience in those places, we must let down our defenses and welcome the *when* to come in and do the work for which it was purposed. We must trust God that, no matter how difficult this season is, it will be of benefit to us because it came from Him.

The next step to embracing is to "hug" or "clasp". In embracing a person or entity, we have opened our arms and allowed that person or entity to enter our "personal space." To continue the embracing, we must now close our arms and "squeeze" the person or entity, being careful not to squeeze too hard. In doing so, for a brief moment we have become "one" with the person or entity. This brief moment is a period of intimacy and sharing. We come to learn intricate personal revelations about people during hugging.

Therefore, when we embrace a *when*, we must also "clasp" or "hug" it. To embrace a *when* means that we have now become one with that *when*. We have accepted that season as part of the "grand scheme of things" in our spiritual life. We have become intimate with it and now know intricate facets of it. For a brief period, it has become "us", and we have become "it." It is not that we are dwelling on the spiritual place that we are in, but, at this moment, we "have a hold on" exactly where we are with God and what He is saying to us. This phase of embracing is essential to our being prepared to minister to others that may later experience this *when*.

The third step in physical embracing is releasing the person or entity at the appropriate time. That is, we must know when to let go. Something innate tells us when it is time to release a person whom we are hugging. We understand that the intimate moment has ended and it is time to stop clasping the person. Failure to do so results in an awkward, uncomfortable feeling on the part of one or both parties in the embrace. When the embrace is complete, we open up our arms and release the person or entity.

Likewise, at the completion of embracing of a *when*, we must release it. Because we have previously named the *when*, we understand its purpose for our lives. Therefore, at this point of the embrace, we should realize that its purpose has been fulfilled. Once we know that that season has passed and everything that was to be accomplished was done, we must then "let it go." Too often we get stuck in a rut, staying in the same spiritual place for a long period of time. Because we embrace *whens*, we become familiar with them. As a result, we get too comfortable with it for too long of a period of time. God may be wanting us to go on to something else, but we are still stuck in one place.

An example of this can be heard in the testimonies of many Believers who, for many years, have the same testimony about what God is doing in their lives. Granted, there is nothing wrong in being able to recount what God did for us or taught us 20 years ago. But, to not be able to testify to anything different or new that God has done for us than He did for us 20 years ago indicates that there has been very little spiritual growth. This scenario occurs because, within 20 years, we have held on to the last thing He taught us. We learned what He taught us 20 years ago, but we got caught up in learning it. Twenty years ago, we embraced that teaching — that season of learning — that *when*. But, based on our testimony of 20 years later, *we have yet to release it*. In not releasing the when at the appropriate time, we stunt our spiritual growth and derail our spiritual walk. It is not until we release a *when* that we can complete our embracing of it. In doing so, we open ourselves up to embrace the next *when*, thereby growing in the spirit and moving closer to God's Divine Purpose for our lives.

Remembering When

Finally, after recognizing, naming and embracing the *when*, we are now able to *remember* the *when*. This means that, at times in which we are going through similar situations or *when*, we are ministering to someone who is going through the same *when*, we can look back on our when and extrapolate the lessons learned during that *when*. The blessing in being able to remember the *when* is two-fold: First, it allows us to not make mistakes that we have made during previous *whens*, thus not retarding our spiritual growth. Secondly, it allows us to help others who are in need of the experiences that we have.

"But," one might ask, "what about Philippians 3:13b-14?" This passage of scripture says "...forgetting those things which are behind me, and reaching forth unto those things which are before, I press toward the mark for the prize of the high calling of God in Christ Jesus"? Does the idea of remembering the *when* conflict with these verses? No. In this passage of scripture, Paul was making the point that it is not wise or beneficial to dwell on the past (i.e., as happens when we do not let go at the end of the embrace). Instead, he pressed "toward the mark for the prize of the high calling." Instead, Paul strived to not become stagnated by trying to relive past times. Paul was not telling the Philippians not to learn from their past (i.e., remember their when). He was simply telling them that in pressing toward the mark He recognized that there is "life after the *when*". Therefore, **remembering** *when* and **dwelling in the past are not the same thing.**

When we remember our *whens*, we draw upon the things we have learned. If we are wise, we learn to thank God for our *whens*, no matter how difficult they were or how long it took us to get what God was trying to show us. It may have occurred "in the twinkling of an eye"; it may have taken a "three-day's journey"; it may have cost us "40 years in the wilderness." But, the important thing is that we grasped the lesson for which the *when* was appointed to teach us.

In reminiscing about this season in our lives, we may remember many things. For instance, we may remember any heartache we experienced during this time. We may also remember various obstacles that we encountered. However, in remembering our *whens*, we must be cognizant of the fact that there is no such thing as a "bad" *when*. We understand that this is true because "we know that all things work together for the good to them who love the Lord and who are the called according to His purpose" (Romans 8:28). Therefore, whether a *when* was pleasant or unpleasant is of no consequence. *All whens are ultimately good* because they help us to get to the next level in God. Therefore, in remembering a *when*, we must realize that no matter what happened during that season, God was there and He saw us through it all.

PUTTING IT ALL TOGETHER

How can we then apply the principles of recognizing, naming, embracing and identifying the *when* to our personal spiritual *whens*? To understand this process, let us review the *When* of Prophetic Paradigms and Patterns (*Chapter Four*). In this chapter, I told the story of prophetic dreams I experienced. In these dreams, a dear childhood friend would appear. Through these dreams, God would reveal things to me regarding decisions I was about to make. Below I have used the exact wording as in Chapter Four to relay the story of the dreams. However, our processes we had discussed in this section appear in bolded letters:

"Although the dreams were infrequent, as I began to understand prophetic revelation, I knew that God was trying to speak to me; I *recognized my when*. As I matured in the gift of the prophetic, I understood that this friend would appear in my dreams during times in which I was about to make an important decision of some sort. I realized that I was then in decision mode. After realizing this, I then understood **what specific decision** God was helping me to make — I *named my when*. I came to understand that this was the simplest way that God could relay to me what He was trying to tell me about various decisions in my life, even though the interpretation of these dreams often proved to be somewhat puzzling. Nevertheless, I accepted God's way of speaking to me in this manner — I *embraced my when*. Each time after that, whenever I had a dream in which the friend appeared, I understood that I was in "decision" mode — I *remembered my when*."

IN PURSUIT OF THE WHEN

In writing this book, I have devoted much time and energy to teaching about our spiritual *whens*. I am confident that I have taught both thoroughly and accurately, as I wrote under the Divine Influence and Direction of the Holy Spirit. However, I would not dare presume that I, in this one book, have taught anyone "everything you need to know" about our spiritual *whens*. The pursuit of knowledge about our spiritual seasons is an ongoing process that must be undertaken by each and every Believer. While the concepts and premises are the same for all of us, our personal spiritual seasons affect each of us differently and, as such, must be examined by the individual. In writing this book, I have merely laid the foundation for each reader to conduct a more personal, in-depth inquiry about the spiritual *whens* in his or her life. I concur with Peter when he said, "...Of a truth, I perceive that God is no respecter of persons (Acts 10:34)." He will not stop at revealing these mysteries to me. God wants His People to know where we have been; He wants us to know where we are going. I have no doubt that He will reveal these profound mysteries about the spiritual *whens* to all of us *when* we ask and *when* we are spiritually ready to receive them.

Conclusion

"When I Kept Silence, My Bones Waxed Old Through The Roaring All The Day Long." – **PSALM 32:3**

In concluding *When* — my first book ever and the first book of the *Roaring* series — I am thankful to God for the prophetic revelations He allowed me to share via these pages. I am humbled to be spoken to and taught by a God whose magnificence and awesomeness is not reserved only for the great and powerful, but can be seen even in the minute and obscure — even in a word such as *when*. I am equally humbled that He would choose me "for such a time as this" to impart the deep, hidden mysteries of our *whens* to you, God's anointed and prophetic people. I sincerely hope that, in writing this book in this manner, I have walked worthy of my vocations as a prophet/teacher/author. I pray that this book has been a blessing to you.

Let us now recap what we have learned thus far. In Psalm 32:3 — the source scripture for the *Roaring* series — David begins by using the word *when*. David was referring to a particular spiritual season, one in which the things that were inside of him were literally killing him because they were not being released. In this verse, David did not have any peace because he had not released those things to God. Likewise, God said that if we are to have any peace, we must allow Him to extrapolate all that is within us — both good and bad. If we need it, He will perfect it during our *whens* and give it back to be used for His Glory. If we do not need it, He will cleanse us of it and take it away from us. God wants us to be spiritually astute enough to know what He is doing in a particular *when*. That is, we must be able to *recognize, name, embrace and remember our whens*. If we know the seasons, we understand what God is doing within those times, and with patience, we allow Him to do a "perfect work" within us.

A NINTH WHEN

In the Introduction, I cited the definition of *when* as a noun, which means "the time in which something is done or comes about". I said that this definition applied to the discussion of each spiritual *when* in the following chapters. For example, every time I wrote "the *when*" I was using the word *when* in accordance with this definition. As such, I did not feel led of the Lord to devote an entire chapter to this definition but was satisfied with writing about the eight *whens* we previously discussed. However, as I began to write this Conclusion, God spoke a Prophetic Word to me concerning a "new" *when* — a season of manifestations. This ninth *when* denotes a prophetic season in which the things for which we have believed God will come into fruition. As I close this book and prepare to write *"I Kept Silence"* — the next book in the *Roaring* series — I will leave you with this Prophetic Word concerning *"the time in which something is done or comes about"* — The *When* of Prophetic Manifestations:

God said that, for too long, we have received many promises and prophecies concerning what He is going to do in our lives. As His People, we have learned to believe what He said simply because He said it. But, even with unwavering faith, we have longed to see the manifestation of His Promises; we have yearned to see the fulfillment of His Word. Through trials and unfathomable hardships, we have waited. Through times of uncertainty and attacks of unbelief, we have waited. When it seemed as if we would faint, we yet waited; waited to see the blessings and promises of the Lord manifested in our lives.   We have prayed earnestly and incessantly. We have sought His face. We have kept his ways. We, His People ask, "What more can we do?" In a still, quiet voice, He answers us, saying, "You must wait yet a little while longer."

God said that there is coming a season in which the things for which we have petitioned Him will manifest before our very eyes. This season will be known as the *When* of Prophetic Manifestations. During this *when*, many in the Body of Christ will experience miraculous manifestations as never before. We will be "with one accord" and share a common goal — to magnify God and to build His Kingdom. As we become one with each other and one with Him, there is literally "no good thing" that He will withhold from us. When we enter into this intensely prophetic season, whatever we speak, we will have instantly. Whatever we think will materialize in a matter of moments. Because we will have obtained a unity with the Holy Spirit and its Divine Creative powers: anything we ask will instantly be created in the spirit realm and then instantly manifested in the physical realm. All this, but, God says, we must yet wait.

We must wait until we are spiritually mature enough to receive such power. We must wait until we have learned how to achieve unity with the Body of Christ and with Christ Himself. We must also wait until our desires line up with God's desires for us.

Because of the wait and because of the "criteria", there will be many who have waited previously who will "fall by the wayside" before this season occurs. They will become "weary in well-doing" and will no longer seek for the promises of God but will instead settle for second-best. They will no longer desire to acquire the manifested promises of God — the *"Prophetic Diamonds in the rough"*. Instead, they will settle for *"Carnal Cubic Zirconias"* — the makeshift manifestations of the flesh realm that (momentarily) appease the desires for which we were previously waiting.

However, God said, those who would *embrace* the *When* of Prophetic Manifestations will be those who are tired of second-best. They will be a chosen few who despise generic, quick-fix blessings. This prophetic remnant will be as the "these are they" multitude in the Book of Revelations. They will have "come through great trials and tribulations" in their walk with the Lord. As such, they will have learned to spot the "fakes" a mile away on their spiritual journey. They will have an acquired appreciation for "the genuine article". This called-out Prophetic few will want God's Best and will accept no substitutes — *even if receiving God's best requires them to wait!* God said that it is to these that He will entrust such power. During the *When* of Prophetic Manifestation, it is to these precious few that He will show Himself in a dispensation of power and might that has not been seen in the physical realm since Jesus walked the face of the earth.

www.ingramcontent.com/pod-product-compliance
Lightning Source LLC
Chambersburg PA
CBHW051213090426
42742CB00021B/3444